✓ **W9-BMB-279**

Success With
Reading Tests

New York • Toronto • London • Auckland • Sydney
Mexico City • New Delhi • Hong Kong • Buenos Aires

Teaching *Resources*

The *Scholastic Success With Reading Tests* series is designed to help you help students succeed on standardized tests. In this workbook for third grade, the 15, four-page tests are culled from the reading skills practice tests provided three times a year to *Scholastic News Edition 3* subscribers, with some new and revised material. By familiarizing children with the skills, language, and formats they will encounter on state and national tests like the Terra Nova, ITBS, CTBS, and MAT, these practice tests will boost confidence and help raise scores.

The questions supporting each test are specifically designed to review the following skills:

- Finding the Main Idea
- Reading for Detail
- Understanding Vocabulary
- Making Inferences
- Sequencing
- Understanding Cause and Effect
- Understanding Author's Purpose
- Understanding Fact and Opinion

Note that the tests in the second half of the book are slightly more difficult. These are designed to be given later in the school year.

In addition to helping children prepare for "real" tests, the practice tests in this workbook may be used as a diagnostic tool, to help you detect individual students' strengths and weaknesses, or as an instructional tool, for oral reading and discussion.

Keep in mind that our practice tests are just that—practice. These tests are not standardized. They should not be used to determine grade level, to compare one student's performance with that of others, or to evaluate teachers' abilities.

HOW TO ADMINISTER THE TESTS:

Before administering each test, you may wish to review with students some basic test-taking strategies, such as reading the questions before reading the passages.

- Establish a relaxed atmosphere. Explain to students that they will not be graded and that they are taking the test to practice for "real" tests down the road.
- Review the directions, then read the samples in each section and discuss the answers. Be sure to pay close attention to the directions in the vocabulary or study skills section on the last page of each test.
- To mimic the atmosphere of a real test, you may wish to set time limits. Students should be able to complete the reading comprehension section (the first three pages of each test) in 20 to 25 minutes. Allow an additional 10 minutes for the vocabulary or study skills portion on the last page of each test.
- Use the **Answer Key** provided on pages 63–64 to check students' work; or if desired, have students check their own answers.

State Standards Correlations

To find out how this book helps you meet your state's standards, log on to **www.scholastic.com/ssw**

Cover design by Ka-Yeon Kim-Li

ISBN-13 978-0-545-20103-2
ISBN-10 0-545-20103-9

10   40   17 16 15 14

Reading Skills Practice Test I

READING COMPREHENSION

Read each story. Then fill in the circle that best completes each sentence or answers each question.

SAMPLE

Imagine drinking 500 cups of water at once. Believe it or not, that's what camels do! In the desert, water is hard to find. When a camel finds water, it drinks as much as it can. Because a camel has a big stomach, it can **gulp** down 30 gallons. That's nearly 500 cups. Then it can go for 10 months without another drink.

I. What is the best title for this story?
- ○ **A.** "Why Water Is Good for You"
- ○ **B.** "Life in the Desert"
- ○ **C.** "Thirsty Camels"
- ○ **D.** "Water Pollution"

2. In the story, the word **gulp** means
- ○ **A.** throw.
- ○ **B.** drink.
- ○ **C.** watch.
- ○ **D.** walk.

A. Have you ever heard of the Man in the Moon? Many people say they can see a man's face on the surface of the moon. It's not really a face, of course. Instead, the "face" is a pattern made by **craters** and mountains on the moon's surface. When the moon is full and the sky is clear, we see some of those holes and hills.

I. What is the best title for this story?
- ○ **A.** "The Moon and Stars"
- ○ **B.** "A Full Moon"
- ○ **C.** "People Land on the Moon"
- ○ **D.** "The Man in the Moon"

2. In this story, the word **craters** means
- ○ **A.** holes.
- ○ **B.** moons.
- ○ **C.** mountains.
- ○ **D.** nights.

3. You can see the Man in the Moon best when the moon is
- ○ **A.** hidden.
- ○ **B.** new.
- ○ **C.** full.
- ○ **D.** flat.

4. You would probably find this story in a
- ○ **A.** science book.
- ○ **B.** dictionary.
- ○ **C.** poetry book.
- ○ **D.** travel guide.

B. A fire can be serious. But these few simple tips can help keep you safe:

1. Put a smoke detector on every level of your home. Check the batteries once a month.
2. Make an escape plan with your family. Plan two ways to get out of each room in case of fire. Pick a spot to meet outside. Then practice!
3. If your city does not have 911, know the phone number for the fire department.
4. If there is a fire, feel a door before opening it. If it is warm, do not open it. Use another way out.
5. Crawl low under smoke.
6. If your clothes catch fire, stop and drop to the ground. Roll around to put out the flames.

1. This story is mainly about
- ○ **A.** how most fires start.
- ● **B.** how to stay safe from fire.
- ○ **C.** how to fix a smoke detector.
- ○ **D.** what firefighters do.

2. You should check the batteries in a smoke detector
- ○ **A.** once a year.
- ○ **B.** twice a year.
- ○ **C.** when you think of it.
- ● **D.** once a month.

3. You can guess from the story that a warm door means
- ○ **A.** the fire is over.
- ● **B.** the fire is close by.
- ○ **C.** firefighters are on the way.
- ○ **D.** the fire is small.

4. If your clothes catch fire, what should you do first?
- ● **A.** Stop.
- ○ **B.** Cry.
- ○ **C.** Roll.
- ○ **D.** Run.

C. The President of the United States has one of the toughest jobs in the world. He also has one of the nicest homes.

The President lives in the White House, in Washington, D.C. This **mansion** has 132 rooms, 32 bathrooms, and 3 elevators. It has a swimming pool, a bowling alley, and a movie theater. It even has its own doctor's office and barbershop! That means the President can do a lot without leaving home.

The President's home is so beautiful, it used to be called the "President's Palace." President Theodore Roosevelt named it the White House in 1901.

Do you wish you owned a home like the White House? You already do! According to the U.S. Constitution, the President does not own the White House. The American people do!

1. What is the best title for this story?
- ○ **A.** "Beautiful Homes"
- ○ **B.** "A New President"
- ● **C.** "The President's Home"
- ○ **D.** "Write to the President"

2. In this story, the word **mansion** means a big
- ● **A.** job.   ○ **C.** car.
- ○ **B.** pool.   ● **D.** home.

3. Which of these is an **opinion** about the White House?
- ○ **A.** It's in Washington, D.C.
- ○ **B.** It has 132 rooms.
- ● **C.** It's the nicest house in the world.
- ○ **D.** It has a barbershop.

D. One African folktale tells why some spiders have bald heads. In the tale, Dog, Elephant, and other animals were having a festival to honor their parents. Anansi the spider bragged to the other animals. He said he had the best way to honor his parents. He would go a whole week without eating! The other animals groaned. They knew Anansi was a show-off.

That week, the other animals ate and ate. But Anansi got hungrier and hungrier. One day, he spotted a pot full of beans. "I will take a tiny taste," thought Anansi. "No one will know."

So Anansi took off his hat and filled it with beans. He had just begun to eat when he heard a noise. The other animals were coming! Quickly, Anansi put the hat on his head. But he forgot the hat was full of beans. The hot beans burned all the hair off Anansi's head. The other animals laughed. "Maybe this will teach Anansi to stop bragging," they said.

1. Which happened first?
○ **A.** Anansi ate the beans.
◉ **B.** The beans burned Anansi's head.
○ **C.** Anansi saw the pot.
○ **D.** Anansi filled his hat.

2. The author created this story to tell
○ **A.** that it is good to show off.
○ **B.** how to cook beans.
○ **C.** that it is wrong to brag.
◉ **D.** that beans are tasty.

E. Much of our planet is covered by water. This water is always on the move. It makes a journey called the *water cycle*.

The water cycle starts when the sun's heat warms Earth's oceans and rivers. The heat makes tiny drops of water **rise** into the air. These tiny drops are called *water vapor*.

Next, the tiny drops of water gather together. They form clouds. When the clouds get too heavy, water spills out of them. The water falls back down to Earth as rain or snow. Then, the water begins its journey again.

1. In this story, the word **rise** means
◉ **A.** move up.
○ **B.** move over.
○ **C.** fall.
○ **D.** break.

2. What is the best title for this story?
○ **A.** "Let It Snow!"
○ **B.** "Earth's Oceans"
◉ **C.** "The Water Cycle"
○ **D.** "Types of Clouds"

3. You can guess from the story that
○ **A.** Earth has very little water.
◉ **B.** snow is made of water.
○ **C.** clouds are made of salt.
○ **D.** water never moves.

4. Which of these is a *fact*?
○ **A.** Everyone hates rain.
○ **B.** Snow is better than rain.
○ **C.** Science is boring.
◉ **D.** Drops of water form clouds.

VOCABULARY

Synonyms

Read the underlined word in each phrase. Mark the word below it that has the same (or close to the same) meaning.

Sample:

roam around
- ○ **A.** play
- ○ **B.** wander
- ○ **C.** read
- ○ **D.** see

1. speak loudly
   - ○ **A.** laugh
   - ○ **B.** look
   - ● **C.** talk
   - ○ **D.** bend

2. allow her in
   - ○ **A.** turn
   - ● **B.** let
   - ○ **C.** stand
   - ○ **D.** call

3. a terrible day
   - ○ **A.** slow
   - ● **B.** awful
   - ○ **C.** early
   - ● **D.** old

4. the correct answer
   - ● **A.** right
   - ○ **B.** first
   - ○ **C.** blue
   - ○ **D.** wrong

5. create artwork
   - ○ **A.** none
   - ○ **B.** buy
   - ○ **C.** drop
   - ● **D.** make

6. the fearful boy
   - ○ **A.** gentle
   - ● **B.** scared
   - ○ **C.** silly
   - ○ **D.** kind

7. finish the chore
   - ○ **A.** play
   - ○ **B.** pet
   - ● **C.** job
   - ○ **D.** day

Antonyms

Read the underlined word in each phrase. Mark the word below it that means the opposite or nearly the opposite.

Sample:

a strong person
- ○ **A.** smart
- ○ **B.** new
- ○ **C.** healthy
- ○ **D.** weak

1. a narrow hall
   - ○ **A.** wide
   - ○ **B.** shiny
   - ○ **C.** cool
   - ○ **D.** dry

2. a noisy crowd
   - ○ **A.** neat
   - ○ **B.** lost
   - ○ **C.** quiet
   - ○ **D.** big

3. load the truck
   - ○ **A.** lonely
   - ○ **B.** unload
   - ○ **C.** pack
   - ○ **D.** reload

4. many friends
   - ○ **A.** real
   - ○ **B.** my
   - ○ **C.** few
   - ○ **D.** all

5. a fancy coat
   - ○ **A.** plain
   - ○ **B.** short
   - ○ **C.** soft
   - ○ **D.** cold

6. a useful tool
   - ○ **A.** powerful
   - ○ **B.** wonderful
   - ○ **C.** used
   - ○ **D.** useless

7. a rare animal
   - ○ **A.** common
   - ○ **B.** ugly
   - ○ **C.** wild
   - ○ **D.** oily

Reading Skills Practice Test 2

READING COMPREHENSION

Read each story. Then fill in the circle that best completes each sentence or answers each question.

SAMPLE

Did you ever hear someone say, "I'd do it at the drop of a hat"? The person means he or she would do it right away. This saying started hundreds of years ago. Back then, people would drop a hat in order to start a race. When the hat touched the ground, the runners would take off. Today, we use the **phrase** "at the drop of a hat" when a person does something suddenly or eagerly.

1. What is the best title for this story?
- ○ **A.** "Races of Long Ago"
- ○ **B.** "At the Drop of a Hat"
- ○ **C.** "Hat Styles"
- ○ **D.** "Who Will Win?"

2. In this story, the word **phrase** means
- ○ **A.** runner.
- ○ **B.** hat.
- ○ **C.** saying.
- ○ **D.** name.

A. To a bat, the world must seem topsy-turvy. That's because this creature spends a good part of its day hanging upside down! A bat has five sharp claws on each of its short **hind** legs. It uses the claws to hang upside down from tree branches, caves, and city bridges. A bat hangs for many hours each day—even while it is sleeping, eating, and washing itself. In fact, the only time this flying mammal is right side up is when it is fetching insects, fruit, or other meals.

1. This story is mainly about
- ○ **A.** how bats find food.
- ◉ **B.** how bats hang upside down.
- ○ **C.** bats and other mammals.
- ○ **D.** all kinds of caves.

2. In this story, the word **hind** means
- ○ **A.** flying.
- ○ **B.** imaginary.
- ◉ **C.** dry.
- ○ **D.** back.

3. Bats are right side up when they
- ○ **A.** find food.
- ◉ **B.** sleep.
- ○ **C.** wash themselves.
- ○ **D.** eat.

4. You can guess from the story that bats
- ○ **A.** never leave their caves or trees.
- ○ **B.** are very dirty animals.
- ◉ **C.** eat only insects.
- ○ **D.** live in the city and the country.

B.   In the 1620s, Pilgrim children had plenty of work to do in the new settlement. They studied, hunted for food, prepared meals, and helped care for younger brothers and sisters. But these early American kids had some time for fun, too. One of their favorite games was called Puss in the Middle. Would you like to play this Pilgrim game? Just follow the directions below:

1. Gather four friends. Have one child stand in the middle of the room. He or she is Puss.
2. Have the other four children stand in the corners of the room.
3. The corner players must change places without giving Puss a chance to grab a corner spot.
4. When Puss gets a corner spot, the child who lost his or her spot becomes the next Puss. The game starts all over again!

1. This story is mainly about
   ○ **A.** how to play a Pilgrim game.
   ○ **B.** how the Pilgrims came to America.
   ○ **C.** foods the Pilgrims ate.
   ○ **D.** what Pilgrim kids studied.

2. Pilgrim children played Puss in the
   ○ **A.** 1800s.   ○ **C.** 1500s.
   ○ **B.** 1600s.   ○ **D.** 1900s.

3. To play Puss in the Middle, what should you do first?
   ○ **A.** Try to change places.
   ○ **B.** Stand in the corners.
   ○ **C.** Have Puss stand in the middle.
   ○ **D.** Gather four friends.

4. Which of these is an *opinion* about Pilgrim children?
   ○ **A.** They played silly games.
   ○ **B.** They helped prepare meals.
   ○ **C.** They lived in the Colonies.
   ○ **D.** They hunted for food.

C.   For many kids, there is nothing like a good action movie. They love seeing their favorite stars **leap** across rooftops or drive at high speeds in a thrilling chase. What they may not know is that, behind every dangerous scene, there is a stunt person. Stunt people look like the real movie stars, but they are specially trained to perform daring tricks. They practice dangerous scenes over and over again. And they wear thick padding on their backs, arms, and shoulders to protect themselves.

Stunt people use other safety tricks, too. When they must fall during a scene, they often land on a mattress or trampoline. When a car window explodes in the stunt person's face, it is made of fake glass that will not cut the skin. Although you can't see these tricks on camera, they sure help keep you glued to the screen!

1. What is the best title for this story?
   ○ **A.** "Kids' Favorite Movie Stars"
   ○ **B.** "Dangerous Jobs"
   ○ **C.** "How Stunt People Work"
   ○ **D.** "Action Movies"

2. In this story the word **leap** means
   ○ **A.** jump.   ○ **C.** land.
   ○ **B.** skip.   ○ **D.** practice.

3. Movie makers use fake glass because
   ○ **A.** it is cheaper than real glass.
   ○ **B.** it breaks easily.
   ○ **C.** it won't cut the skin.
   ○ **D.** it is easy to get.

4. You might find this story in
   ○ **A.** a book about movies.
   ○ **B.** an encyclopedia.
   ○ **C.** a nature guide.
   ○ **D.** a book about planes.

D. One African folktale tells how Leopard got his spots. According to the tale, Leopard and some other animals had a funeral march for their friend Ant. As the animals walked, Leopard's stomach rumbled. He was hungry!

As the animals passed a farm, Leopard noticed some baskets filled with fresh eggs. He tossed one egg after another into his mouth. Soon he had eaten an entire basket! Satisfied, he returned to the other animals.

When the farmer saw the empty basket, he chased after the animals. "Who stole my eggs?" he asked. All of the animals denied it. Then the farmer had an idea. He asked all the animals to jump over a bonfire. He said the animal who had eaten the eggs would fall in. One by one, the creatures leaped over the flames. When it was Leopard's turn, he took a deep breath, jumped, and landed in the fire. "Aha!" said the farmer. "It was you!" Leopard climbed out of the fire, but his coat was burned in spots as a reminder of his greed.

I. Which happened last?
- ○ **A.** Leopard ate the eggs.
- ○ **B.** Leopard burned his coat.
- ○ **C.** Leopard was hungry.
- ○ **D.** The farmer saw the empty basket.

2. The author created this story to tell
- ○ **A.** that it is bad to steal.
- ○ **B.** how to make music.
- ○ **C.** how leopards live.
- ○ **D.** all about Africa.

3. You can guess that
- ○ **A.** African animals can talk.
- ○ **B.** this event never really happened.
- ○ **C.** ants are very smart.
- ○ **D.** leopards are allergic to eggs.

E. To author Joanna Cole, writing about science is a dream come true. When Cole was growing up in New Jersey, she explored nature. She grew gardens and caught bugs in her yard.

When Cole grew up, she became a teacher. One day, she saw an article about cockroaches. She learned that these bugs are older than dinosaurs. She thought kids would like to learn about roaches, too. She decided to write a book about them. Later, Cole wrote books about fish, fleas, frogs, dogs, and more. Of course, some of Cole's most famous books are the *Magic School Bus* science stories.

No matter what she is writing about, Cole says that two things are important to her. One is research. Cole reads many books and talks to experts to make sure her facts are **correct**. The second thing is a sense of humor. She says even science should be funny!

I. In this story, the word **correct** means
- ○ **A.** fix.   ○ **C.** funny.
- ○ **B.** new.   ○ **D.** right.

2. This story would probably go on to talk about
- ○ **A.** the success of Cole's books.
- ○ **B.** cockroaches and dinosaurs.
- ○ **C.** kids' hobbies.
- ○ **D.** using the library.

3. What is the best title for this story?
- ○ **A.** "Cockroaches: Ancient Bugs"
- ○ **B.** "Joanna Cole: Science Writer"
- ○ **C.** "The *Magic School Bus* Books"
- ○ **D.** "How to Write a Funny Story"

4. Which of these is a *fact*?
- ○ **A.** Cole is the best author ever.
- ○ **B.** Roaches are gross.
- ○ **C.** Cole grew up in New Jersey.
- ○ **D.** Science is more interesting than art.

VOCABULARY

Synonyms

Read the underlined word in each phrase. Mark the word below it that has the same (or close to the same) meaning.

Sample:

nibble the food
- ○ **A.** see
- ○ **B.** bite
- ○ **C.** fill
- ○ **D.** leave

1. a joyful day
   - ○ **A.** long
   - ○ **B.** new
   - ○ **C.** sad
   - ○ **D.** happy

2. complete the work
   - ○ **A.** forget
   - ○ **B.** know
   - ○ **C.** finish
   - ○ **D.** try

3. an ache in her ear
   - ○ **A.** drop
   - ○ **B.** way
   - ○ **C.** noise
   - ○ **D.** pain

4. a foolish idea
   - ○ **A.** large
   - ○ **B.** old
   - ○ **C.** silly
   - ○ **D.** great

5. plead for food
   - ○ **A.** beg
   - ○ **B.** run
   - ○ **C.** drive
   - ○ **D.** look

6. vanish without a trace
   - ○ **A.** appear
   - ○ **B.** disappear
   - ○ **C.** cry
   - ○ **D.** laugh

7. permit him to go
   - ○ **A.** rush
   - ○ **B.** stop
   - ○ **C.** allow
   - ○ **D.** forbid

Antonyms

Read the underlined word in each phrase. Mark the word below it that means the opposite or nearly the opposite.

Sample:

an ill person
- ○ **A.** small
- ○ **B.** kind
- ○ **C.** healthy
- ○ **D.** sick

1. refuse to go
   - ○ **A.** say
   - ○ **B.** agree
   - ○ **C.** read
   - ○ **D.** fail

2. the worst thing
   - ○ **A.** best
   - ○ **B.** last
   - ○ **C.** first
   - ○ **D.** scariest

3. beneath the table
   - ○ **A.** under
   - ○ **B.** near
   - ○ **C.** above
   - ○ **D.** off

4. a slow trickle
   - ○ **A.** drip
   - ○ **B.** line
   - ○ **C.** gush
   - ○ **D.** day

5. a lively show
   - ○ **A.** dull
   - ○ **B.** expensive
   - ○ **C.** fun
   - ○ **D.** short

6. a difficult test
   - ○ **A.** tricky
   - ○ **B.** exciting
   - ○ **C.** planned
   - ○ **D.** easy

7. an enormous creature
   - ○ **A.** quiet
   - ○ **B.** tiny
   - ○ **C.** wild
   - ○ **D.** fierce

Reading Skills Practice Test 3

READING COMPREHENSION

Read each story. Then fill in the circle that best completes each sentence or answers each question.

SAMPLE

Red-knee tarantula spiders are in trouble. Some people take these spiders from the wild and sell them as pets. Now, scientists hope to save the red-knee tarantula. They think the spider's **venom**, or poison, might be used to cure some diseases.

I. What is the best title for this story?
○ **A.** "The Spider's Knees"
○ **B.** "A Terrific Pet"
○ **C.** "Save the Spiders"
○ **D.** "How to Catch a Spider"

2. In the story, the word **venom** means
○ **A.** poison.
○ **B.** red knee.
○ **C.** tarantula.
○ **D.** disease.

A. Imagine a world where countries work together to solve problems. A group called the United Nations works to make that dream come true. The United Nations, or UN, is made up of 189 countries. It was formed in 1945, after World War II. The countries that started the UN wanted to **prevent** another big war from happening.

Today, the UN still tries to stop wars, but it has other jobs, too. UN workers bring food to people in poor countries. They try to wipe out deadly diseases. They even look for ways to help the environment.

I. The best title for this story is
○ **A.** "All About World War II."
○ **B.** "All About the UN."
○ **C.** "How to Help the Earth."
○ **D.** "How to Stop Wars."

2. Which of these happened last?
○ **A.** The UN was formed.
○ **B.** World War II ended.
○ **C.** World War II started.
○ **D.** The UN began to help poor people.

3. In the story, the word **prevent** means
○ **A.** help.
○ **B.** hungry.
○ **C.** stop.
○ **D.** begin.

4. You can guess from the story that
○ **A.** the UN started World War II.
○ **B.** peace is important to the UN.
○ **C.** the United States does not belong to the UN.
○ **D.** every country in the world belongs to the UN.

B. In the rain forest, orangutans swing from tree to tree all day. Now, they can feel right at home at the National Zoo in Washington, D.C. The zoo has set up a pretend forest. Instead of trees, it has tall towers. Wires called **cables** run between the towers. Orangutans can swing from the cables—just like they would from branches. The zoo's six orangutans swing around the exhibit. Visitors sit in the middle and watch the apes swing overhead.

I. This story is mainly about
  ○ **A.** what orangutans eat.
  ○ **B.** how to build a pretend forest.
  ○ **C.** how the National Zoo has made orangutans feel at home.
  ○ **D.** what visitors can buy at the National Zoo.

2. Instead of trees, the orangutan exhibit has
  ○ **A.** towers.
  ○ **B.** flowers.
  ○ **C.** apes.
  ○ **D.** buildings.

3. In the story, the word **cables** means
  ○ **A.** wires.
  ○ **B.** forests.
  ○ **C.** pretend.
  ○ **D.** monkeys.

4. Which sentence is an *opinion* about orangutans?
  ○ **A.** They swing from tree to tree.
  ○ **B.** They live in forests.
  ○ **C.** They are cute.
  ○ **D.** Six of them live at the National Zoo.

C. He was born in Italy more than 500 years ago. He is known as one of the world's greatest artists. But Leonardo da Vinci might also be one of the smartest people who ever lived.

People who have studied Leonardo's notebooks can't believe what they've found. Leonardo's drawings show that he was a scientist, an astronomer, and an engineer. He had ideas about how waves form, why the moon shines, and how flying machines might work. Though no one knows why, Leonardo wrote all his ideas down backward! You need a mirror to read his writing.

I. The main idea of the story is that Leonardo da Vinci
  ○ **A.** liked watching the moon.
  ○ **B.** may be one of the smartest people who ever lived.
  ○ **C.** lived a very long time ago.
  ○ **D.** was an astronomer.

2. Leonardo da Vinci was born in
  ○ **A.** Italy.   ○ **C.** England.
  ○ **B.** the U.S.   ○ **D.** France.

3. You need a mirror to read Leonardo's writing because
  ○ **A.** he had messy handwriting.
  ○ **B.** he wrote by moonlight.
  ○ **C.** he wrote in pictures instead of words.
  ○ **D.** he wrote backward.

4. You can guess from the story that
  ○ **A.** Leonardo da Vinci could fly.
  ○ **B.** Italy ruled the world 500 years ago.
  ○ **C.** there were no airplanes 500 years ago.
  ○ **D.** people were smarter 500 years ago than they are now.

D. Thousands of years ago, people in Egypt preserved the bodies of their dead and wrapped them in cloth called **linen**. Today, these mummies can tell scientists about how the Egyptians lived. However, scientists have always had a big problem when they tried to study mummies. If they unwrapped a mummy, they would damage it.

Now, scientists have a way to study mummies without unwrapping them. An X-ray machine called a CAT scanner takes pictures of mummies right through their wraps.

The first mummy that scientists scanned was a female Egyptian mummy. The scanner took pictures of her from different angles. Then, a computer put all the pictures together to form a complete image.

I. In the story, the word **linen** means
○ **A.** old.
○ **C.** machine.
○ **B.** cloth.
○ **D.** scientist.

2. Which of these happened first?
○ **A.** Scientists used CAT scanners to study mummies.
○ **B.** Scientists had trouble unwrapping mummies.
○ **C.** People in Egypt preserved dead bodies.
○ **D.** Egyptian mummies were discovered.

3. This story would probably go on to talk about
○ **A.** what scientists learned about the mummies they scanned.
○ **B.** how the CAT scanner was invented.
○ **C.** machines in ancient Egypt.
○ **D.** different kinds of cloth.

4. Which of these is a *fact*?
○ **A.** Mummies are disgusting.
○ **B.** CAT scanners are a great invention.
○ **C.** Mummies are boring.
○ **D.** Mummies can teach scientists about how people lived.

E. Once there was a very fast rabbit. He bragged loudly to all the town about his speed.

Frog was annoyed by Rabbit's bragging. He challenged Rabbit to a race through some swamp grass down to the town pond. Rabbit agreed.

On the day of the race, Frog played a trick. Several of his frog friends were **concealed** in the swamp grass, one big leap apart from one another.

Rabbit ran as fast as he could through the grass, but no matter how fast he ran, Frog was always one jump ahead of him. By the time Rabbit got to the pond, he was running too fast to stop. He fell right into the pond, just as Frog leaped up from behind a rock and shouted, "I am the fastest!"

And that was that.

I. Frog's friends hid
○ **A.** in grass.
○ **C.** on a rock.
○ **B.** under a log.
○ **D.** in a pond.

2. In this story, the word **concealed** probably means
○ **A.** sleeping.
○ **C.** hidden.
○ **B.** swamp.
○ **D.** all.

3. You would probably find this story in
○ **A.** a book about frogs.
○ **B.** a book of folktales.
○ **C.** a book about running.
○ **D.** a book about swamp life.

4. This story was probably created to tell
○ **A.** where frogs live.
○ **B.** why bragging is a bad idea.
○ **C.** a few facts about rabbits.
○ **D.** all about ponds.

VOCABULARY

Synonyms

Read the underlined word in each phrase. Mark the word below it that has the same (or close to the same) meaning.

Sample:

damage the building
- ○ **A.** hurt
- ○ **B.** give
- ○ **C.** paint
- ○ **D.** roof

1. enormous balloon
   - ○ **A.** shiny
   - ○ **B.** red
   - ○ **C.** huge
   - ○ **D.** instant

2. wild blizzard
   - ○ **A.** storm
   - ○ **B.** sunset
   - ○ **C.** monster
   - ○ **D.** candy

3. angry child
   - ○ **A.** smile
   - ○ **B.** happy
   - ○ **C.** kid
   - ○ **D.** mad

4. sly thief
   - ○ **A.** angry
   - ○ **B.** sneaky
   - ○ **C.** quick
   - ○ **D.** robber

5. appear instantly
   - ○ **A.** disappear
   - ○ **B.** work
   - ○ **C.** climb
   - ○ **D.** show up

6. awoke late
   - ○ **A.** away
   - ○ **B.** woke up
   - ○ **C.** ran
   - ○ **D.** let out

7. choose wisely
   - ○ **A.** never
   - ○ **B.** eat
   - ○ **C.** think
   - ○ **D.** pick

8. the entire time
   - ○ **A.** dinner
   - ○ **B.** lost
   - ○ **C.** whole
   - ○ **D.** wasted

Antonyms

Read the underlined word in each phrase. Mark the word below it that means the opposite or nearly the opposite.

Sample:

silent evening
- ○ **A.** noisy
- ○ **B.** quiet
- ○ **C.** patient
- ○ **D.** perfect

1. rare coin
   - ○ **A.** unusual
   - ○ **B.** money
   - ○ **C.** common
   - ○ **D.** copper

2. lead the troops
   - ○ **A.** hire
   - ○ **B.** metal
   - ○ **C.** mail
   - ○ **D.** follow

3. expensive jewels
   - ○ **A.** cheap
   - ○ **B.** sparkly
   - ○ **C.** diamond
   - ○ **D.** precious

4. narrow path
   - ○ **A.** rocky
   - ○ **B.** trail
   - ○ **C.** dirt
   - ○ **D.** wide

5. foolish person
   - ○ **A.** funny
   - ○ **B.** smart
   - ○ **C.** wealthy
   - ○ **D.** human

6. darkened room
   - ○ **A.** living
   - ○ **B.** lighted
   - ○ **C.** painted
   - ○ **D.** small

7. danger signs
   - ○ **A.** stop
   - ○ **B.** funny
   - ○ **C.** safety
   - ○ **D.** animal

8. beneath the ground
   - ○ **A.** above
   - ○ **B.** near
   - ○ **C.** beside
   - ○ **D.** walk

Reading Skills Practice Test 4

READING COMPREHENSION

Read each story. Then fill in the circle that best completes each sentence or answers each question.

SAMPLE

Your nose and mouth are an open door to germs. But your tonsils stop germs before they get too far. Tonsils are like little sponges inside your throat. They soak up and **destroy** germs.

1. What is the best title for this story?
○ **A.** "How to Be Healthy"
○ **B.** "Keep Your Nose Clean"
○ **C.** "How Your Tonsils Help You"
○ **D.** "Germs Are Bad for You"

2. In this story, the word **destroy** means
○ **A.** hide.
○ **B.** kill.
○ **C.** see.
○ **D.** run.

A. Manatees are large water mammals. They have lived in the ocean near Florida for millions of years. But today, manatees are in danger of dying out. Many manatees get hit by motorboats. Some get tangled in fishing nets. Other manatees get sick in the winter when the water turns cold. Some scientists in Florida want to save the manatees. They have set up a special center where they take care of sick and **injured** manatees. They also rescue baby manatees whose mothers have died.

1. What is the main idea of this story?
○ **A.** Manatees are in danger of dying out.
○ **B.** Some baby manatees need mothers.
○ **C.** Winter makes the ocean turn cold.
○ **D.** Manatees are friendly.

2. Manatees are sometimes hit by
○ **A.** scientists.
○ **B.** fishing poles.
○ **C.** ocean waves.
○ **D.** motorboats.

3. In this story, the word **injured** means
○ **A.** wet.
○ **B.** hurt.
○ **C.** playful.
○ **D.** healthy.

B. Who Has Seen the Wind?

Who has seen the wind?
  Neither I nor you:
But when the leaves hang **trembling**
  The wind is passing through.

Who has seen the wind?
  Neither you nor I:
But when the trees bow down their heads,
  The wind is passing by.

By Christina Rossetti

I. In this poem, the word **trembling** means
  ○ **A.** shaking.   ○ **C.** falling.
  ○ **B.** green.   ○ **D.** still.

2. The leaves tremble because
  ○ **A.** they are afraid.
  ○ **B.** the wind is blowing on them.
  ○ **C.** they are cold.
  ○ **D.** they are about to dry up and fall off the tree.

3. In the poem, the trees bow down their
  ○ **A.** leaves.   ○ **C.** trunks.
  ○ **B.** tops.   ○ **D.** roots.

4. You would probably find this poem in
  ○ **A.** a book about weather.
  ○ **B.** a book of poetry.
  ○ **C.** a science book.
  ○ **D.** a book about trees.

C. Chief Crazy Horse was a Native American hero. In the 1870s, he protected his people from settlers who tried to take their land. Many years after Crazy Horse died, some Native Americans decided to honor him. They hired an artist to carve a giant sculpture of Chief Crazy Horse.

In 1948, the artist started carving the sculpture. He carved into a mountain in South Dakota, using a drill and dynamite. The artist died in 1982. His sculpture of Crazy Horse was not finished. But his family and other workers are finishing the sculpture.

When it is done, it will probably be the largest sculpture in the world.

I. What is the best title for this story?
  ○ **A.** "Mountains of South Dakota"
  ○ **B.** "Native American Chiefs"
  ○ **C.** "A Clay Sculpture"
  ○ **D.** "Sculpture of a Hero"

2. Who began carving the sculpture?
  ○ **A.** Chief Crazy Horse
  ○ **B.** an artist
  ○ **C.** the chief's grandchild
  ○ **D.** a mountain climber

3. Which happened last?
  ○ **A.** Crazy Horse died.
  ○ **B.** An artist began carving a sculpture of Crazy Horse.
  ○ **C.** Some Native Americans decided to honor Crazy Horse.
  ○ **D.** The artist died.

4. Which of these is an *opinion* about Chief Crazy Horse?
  ○ **A.** He protected his people from settlers.
  ○ **B.** He was Native American.
  ○ **C.** He was the bravest chief of all.
  ○ **D.** He was alive during the 1870s.

D.   One fine summer day, some ants were hauling grain into their anthill. They were working hard to store enough grain for winter. A **merry** grasshopper came along, hopping and jumping around. He laughed at the ants. "Why are you working on such a nice day?" he asked. "You should be playing like me."

   Soon, winter came. The ants had plenty to eat. One day, the grasshopper came along, looking very sad. He asked the ants to give him some grain. But the ants just laughed. "Why should we?" they said. "You played all summer while we worked hard. Now you'll go hungry while we eat."

I.   In this story, the word **merry** means
   ○ **A.** sad.
   ○ **B.** ugly.
   ○ **C.** happy.
   ○ **D.** funny.

2.   What is the main idea of this story?
   ○ **A.** All ants are hard workers.
   ○ **B.** Working hard and planning ahead are important.
   ○ **C.** Ants and grasshoppers don't get along very well.
   ○ **D.** It's important to have fun in the summertime.

3.   You can guess from this story that
   ○ **A.** the grasshopper was lazy.
   ○ **B.** the ants didn't like to have fun.
   ○ **C.** real ants eat nothing but grain.
   ○ **D.** grasshoppers live in meadows.

4.   What happened first?
   ○ **A.** Winter came.
   ○ **B.** The ants stored grain.
   ○ **C.** The ants laughed at the grasshopper.
   ○ **D.** The grasshopper asked the ants for some grain.

E.   Most people agree that trees look nice. But trees can also help cities save money. A few years ago, the U.S. Forest Service studied trees in Chicago, Illinois. They learned that just one tree can save a city $402 over the tree's lifetime.

   One way trees save money is by helping us save energy. Trees shade buildings from the summer sun. They also block the winter wind. That cuts down on the energy needed to heat and cool homes and offices. Saving energy means lower bills.

   Here is another way trees can help a city save money. When it rains, a city's sewers fill up with water. Cities spend lots of money to clean that water. But trees' leaves and roots soak up rainwater before it gets to the dirty sewers. With the help of trees, there is less water to clean.

I.   What is the main idea of this story?
   ○ **A.** Trees are pretty.
   ○ **B.** Trees block winter wind.
   ○ **C.** Air pollution costs money.
   ○ **D.** Trees help save money.

2.   This story would probably go on to talk about
   ○ **A.** how to plant flowers.
   ○ **B.** how to get cities to plant more trees.
   ○ **C.** the best way to chop down a tree.
   ○ **D.** forest fires.

3.   Which is a *fact* about trees?
   ○ **A.** Trees look nice.
   ○ **B.** The tallest trees are found in cities.
   ○ **C.** Trees can shade sun and block wind.
   ○ **D.** People should plant more trees.

VOCABULARY

Synonyms

Read the underlined word in each phrase.
Mark the word below it that has the
same (or close to the same) meaning.

Sample:

sip lemonade
- ○ **A.** pour
- ○ **B.** drink
- ○ **C.** make
- ○ **D.** sweet

1. speed away
   - ○ **A.** race
   - ○ **B.** walk
   - ○ **C.** far
   - ○ **D.** fast

2. gentle touch
   - ○ **A.** sharp
   - ○ **B.** cold
   - ○ **C.** soft
   - ○ **D.** finger

3. grumpy neighbor
   - ○ **A.** friendly
   - ○ **B.** tall
   - ○ **C.** grouchy
   - ○ **D.** woman

4. steam carrots
   - ○ **A.** chop
   - ○ **B.** rabbit
   - ○ **C.** eat
   - ○ **D.** cook

5. loud groan
   - ○ **A.** sound
   - ○ **B.** laugh
   - ○ **C.** moan
   - ○ **D.** odor

6. enormous building
   - ○ **A.** big
   - ○ **B.** tired
   - ○ **C.** urban
   - ○ **D.** dark

7. moist washcloth
   - ○ **A.** purple
   - ○ **B.** shower
   - ○ **C.** damp
   - ○ **D.** dirty

Antonyms

Read the underlined word in each phrase.
Mark the word below it that means the
opposite or nearly the opposite.

Sample:

huge truck
- ○ **A.** large
- ○ **B.** red
- ○ **C.** fast
- ○ **D.** tiny

1. begin reading
   - ○ **A.** finish
   - ○ **B.** read
   - ○ **C.** hard
   - ○ **D.** start

2. pleasant weather
   - ○ **A.** nice
   - ○ **B.** sunny
   - ○ **C.** outdoors
   - ○ **D.** stormy

3. feel grief
   - ○ **A.** sadness
   - ○ **B.** comfortable
   - ○ **C.** happiness
   - ○ **D.** winter

4. shallow water
   - ○ **A.** fresh
   - ○ **B.** deep
   - ○ **C.** pool
   - ○ **D.** cold

5. hind leg
   - ○ **A.** back
   - ○ **B.** furry
   - ○ **C.** front
   - ○ **D.** arm

6. visible stain
   - ○ **A.** messy
   - ○ **B.** invisible
   - ○ **C.** cold
   - ○ **D.** new

7. sink in the water
   - ○ **A.** trip
   - ○ **B.** run
   - ○ **C.** bathe
   - ○ **D.** float

Reading Skills Practice Test 5

READING COMPREHENSION

Read each story. Then fill in the circle that best completes each sentence or answers each question.

SAMPLE

Weather experts use information from space to predict the weather on Earth. How? Satellites in space take pictures of Earth's atmosphere. The pictures show experts where storms are **brewing**.

I. The story is mainly about
- ○ **A.** serious hurricanes.
- ○ **B.** weather satellites.
- ○ **C.** our solar system.
- ○ **D.** rockets.

2. In the story, the word **brewing** means
- ○ **A.** finishing.
- ○ **B.** learning.
- ○ **C.** forming.
- ○ **D.** dripping.

A. Do you know how the states got their names? Many names come from Native American words. The word Utah comes from "Ute," the name of a Native American **tribe**. The name Wyoming comes from a Native American word meaning "large prairie."

Other states have names that tell how the states got started. For example, Georgia was named after King George II of England. He started the colony that became Georgia.

I. The best title for this story is
- ○ **A.** "King George II."
- ○ **B.** "Native American Tribes."
- ○ **C.** "Wyoming's Prairie Land."
- ○ **D.** "How States Got Their Names."

2. In the story, the word **tribe** means
- ○ **A.** state.
- ○ **B.** name.
- ○ **C.** group.
- ○ **D.** person.

3. You can guess from the story that
- ○ **A.** the Ute people lived in the area we now call Utah.
- ○ **B.** there are 48 states.
- ○ **C.** the name Georgia comes from a Native American word for "king."
- ○ **D.** the word Florida is French.

4. The story would probably go on to talk about
- ○ **A.** rivers in the United States.
- ○ **B.** other ways states were named.
- ○ **C.** the kings and queens of England.
- ○ **D.** languages of the world.

B. Do your feet stink after you exercise? The bad smell comes from microbes, or living things that grow on your skin. Microbes are very small. You can only see them with a microscope. But they have big names. One is called **corybacteria**.

Microbes are all over your body. But they grow best on skin that is sweaty and warm. That's why feet smell after you exercise.

I. This story is mainly about
  ○ **A.** why you exercise.
  ○ **B.** why feet smell.
  ○ **C.** how to use a microscope.
  ○ **D.** how microbes are named.

2. **Corybacteria** is a kind of
  ○ **A.** sneaker.   ○ **C.** kid.
  ○ **B.** exercise.   ○ **D.** microbe.

3. Your feet smell because
  ○ **A.** microbes grow on them.
  ○ **B.** you use old soap.
  ○ **C.** they are too big.
  ○ **D.** they are funny looking.

4. You can guess from the story that
  ○ **A.** exercise is bad for your health.
  ○ **B.** there are microbes on your face and hands.
  ○ **C.** you should wash your feet three times a day.
  ○ **D.** microbes are green and slimy.

C. Once, only kids at private schools wore uniforms. Now, many public schools ask students to wear uniforms. It has caused a big debate.

Many students like wearing uniforms. They say it is easy to get dressed in the morning. And families have to buy only one or two uniforms, instead of a closet full of clothes.

Not everyone likes school uniforms, though. Some people say it's not fair to make kids wear the same thing.

I. The main idea of the story is that school uniforms
  ○ **A.** are more expensive than regular clothes.
  ○ **B.** are less expensive than regular clothes.
  ○ **C.** have caused a big debate.
  ○ **D.** look nice.

2. Today, uniforms are worn
  ○ **A.** only at private schools.
  ○ **B.** only at public schools.
  ○ **C.** at many private and public schools.
  ○ **D.** only in other countries.

3. The author probably wrote this story to
  ○ **A.** persuade students to wear uniforms.
  ○ **B.** give both sides of the uniform debate.
  ○ **C.** stop children from wearing uniforms.
  ○ **D.** help schools create new uniforms.

D. The story of Paul Bunyan is a famous American legend. It was first told in the early 1900s.

According to the legend, Paul Bunyan was a giant. Paul's parents knew he was going to be big right from the start. When he was only one week old, he wore his father's clothes! He would eat 40 bowls of porridge at one meal.

For his first birthday, Paul got a **huge** blue ox named Babe. Babe and Paul played in the woods. They were so heavy that their footprints formed lakes.

When Paul grew up, he became a lumberjack. He could cut down a whole forest by himself. Once, he formed the Grand Canyon by dragging his tools behind him!

I. In the story, the word **huge** means
○ **A.** large.   ○ **C.** blue.
○ **B.** hungry.   ○ **D.** smart.

2. Which of these happened first?
○ **A.** Paul became a lumberjack.
○ **B.** Paul wore his father's clothes.
○ **C.** Paul formed the Grand Canyon.
○ **D.** Paul got a blue ox.

3. You can guess that
○ **A.** Paul Bunyan lived in Florida.
○ **B.** Paul Bunyan lived in 1850.
○ **C.** the legend is not really true.
○ **D.** footprints can form lakes.

4. Which of these is a fact?
○ **A.** Paul Bunyan was cool.
○ **B.** Legends are very interesting.
○ **C.** It would be fun to have an ox.
○ **D.** A legend is a story.

E. Riding a bike can be fun, but it's important to stay safe. Here are some tips for safe cycling:

- Always wear a bicycle helmet that fits your head. If you fall, it can protect your head from serious injuries.
- Never ride a bike after dark.
- If you are under age 10, do not ride in the street without an adult. When you do ride in the street, use hand signals to show where you are going. Obey stop signs and other traffic rules.
- Wear bright clothing when you ride so that drivers, walkers, and other bicyclists can **spot** you.
- Do not ride a bike that is too large for you, or one that is not in good working order.

I. The story is mainly about
○ **A.** traffic rules.   ○ **C.** bike safety.
○ **B.** tricycles.   ○ **D.** sports.

2. Bike riders should wear clothes that are
○ **A.** bright.   ○ **C.** loose.
○ **B.** tight.   ○ **D.** dark.

3. In the story, the word **spot** means
○ **A.** see.   ○ **C.** dog.
○ **B.** mark.   ○ **D.** help.

4. You would probably find this story in a book about
○ **A.** driving.
○ **B.** safety.
○ **C.** a dictionary.
○ **D.** folk tales.

VOCABULARY

Synonyms

Read the underlined word in each phrase. Mark the word below it that has the same (or close to the same) meaning.

Sample:

speak loudly
- A. look
- B. fly
- C. talk
- D. cry

1. shut the door
   - A. ring
   - B. knock
   - C. open
   - D. close

2. giant creature
   - A. tiny
   - B. scary
   - C. large
   - D. animal

3. reply soon
   - A. return
   - B. swim
   - C. answer
   - D. mind

4. shall go
   - A. will
   - B. never
   - C. please
   - D. back

5. intelligent student
   - A. new
   - B. smart
   - C. alone
   - D. old

6. wander around
   - A. fold
   - B. roam
   - C. soak
   - D. let

7. shred paper
   - A. raise
   - B. news
   - C. rip
   - D. draw

8. chuckle quietly
   - A. laugh
   - B. drink
   - C. whistle
   - D. wash

Antonyms

Read the underlined word in each phrase. Mark the word below it that means the opposite or nearly the opposite.

Sample:

lay asleep
- A. fast
- B. worried
- C. still
- D. awake

1. straight line
   - A. nice
   - B. crooked
   - C. dark
   - D. lost

2. wrong answer
   - A. check
   - B. mark
   - C. right
   - D. last

3. sweet taste
   - A. sugary
   - B. sour
   - C. chocolate
   - D. cold

4. terrible day
   - A. great
   - B. bad
   - C. long
   - D. early

5. frown on her face
   - A. spill
   - B. mad
   - C. smile
   - D. nose

6. tight coat
   - A. loose
   - B. blue
   - C. warm
   - D. small

7. worst thing
   - A. stop
   - B. best
   - C. kind
   - D. past

8. true story
   - A. false
   - B. long
   - C. mine
   - D. near

Reading Skills Practice Test 6

READING COMPREHENSION

Read each story. Then fill in the circle that best completes each sentence or answers each question.

SAMPLE

You can guess the meaning of some words by the way the words sound. For example, the word "squeak" sounds like a squeak. The word "cackle" sounds like a person cackling. These words are called "sound words." It is fun to use sound words when you write.

I. The best title for this story is
○ **A.** "Be a Good Writer."
○ **B.** "Using a Dictionary."
○ **C.** "Sound Words."
○ **D.** "Rhyming Words."

2. You can guess from the story that
_____ is a sound word.
○ **A.** "hiss"   ○ **C.** "spoon"
○ **B.** "plant"   ○ **D.** "sister"

A.   Everyone knows about the telephone, the car, and the electric light. People use these inventions every day. But there are other inventions that few people have heard of. For example, one inventor **created** a twirling fork to make it easier to eat spaghetti. Another invented diapers for pet birds. And someone else invented a sleeping bag with leg holes. Why? The holes let a camper run away when a bear comes along!

I. A good title for this story is
○ **A.** "More Spaghetti!"
○ **B.** "Unusual Inventions."
○ **C.** "Famous Inventions."
○ **D.** "Pet Supplies."

2. In the story, the word **created** means
○ **A.** ate.
○ **B.** ran away.
○ **C.** twirled.
○ **D.** made.

3. You can guess from the story that
○ **A.** more people own cars than twirling forks.
○ **B.** most people have twirling forks.
○ **C.** all campers hate bears.
○ **D.** the person who invented bird diapers is famous.

4. Which of these is an *opinion*?
○ **A.** People use telephones and cars.
○ **B.** Someone invented a twirling fork.
○ **C.** It's silly to make diapers for pets.
○ **D.** Some sleeping bags have leg holes.

B.   Imagine giving stitches to sheep or taking a tiger's temperature. That's what a veterinarian, or animal doctor, does.

There are 60,000 veterinarians in the United States. Some take care of pets like dogs, cats, and hamsters. Others care for farm animals like horses and cows. Still other vets work at zoos. They get to work with elephants, zebras, gorillas, and other unusual creatures.

Being a vet is not easy. Veterinarians go to college for at least eight years to learn about animals. They often work more than 50 hours a week. But many animal doctors say that their **career** is exciting and fun.

I.   How many veterinarians are in the U.S.?
○ **A.** 12,000
○ **B.** 40,000
○ **C.** 60,000
○ **D.** 90,000

2.   In the story, the word **career** means
○ **A.** job.
○ **B.** cat.
○ **C.** patient.
○ **D.** stitches.

3.   Being a vet is hard because a vet often
○ **A.** does not go to college.
○ **B.** works many hours a week.
○ **C.** does not earn any money.
○ **D.** hates dogs and cats.

C.   In February of 1962, John Glenn made space history. This American astronaut climbed aboard a tiny space capsule called the *Friendship 7*. He traveled 160 miles above Earth. Glenn orbited the planet three times, then safely returned to Earth. He had become the first American astronaut to circle the Earth.

In October of 1998, John Glenn made history again. At the age of 77, Glenn became the oldest person ever to fly in space. Glenn blasted into space on board the space shuttle *Discovery*. Glenn's adventure showed space scientists how space travel affects older people.

I.   This story is mostly about
○ **A.** space missions of the 1960s.
○ **B.** astronauts of today.
○ **C.** John Glenn's space flights.
○ **D.** different kinds of spacecraft.

2.   When did Glenn travel on the *Friendship 7*?
○ **A.** October of 1962
○ **B.** October of 1998
○ **C.** February of 1962
○ **D.** February of 1998

3.   Which happened last?
○ **A.** Glenn traveled on the *Discovery*.
○ **B.** Glenn climbed on board the *Friendship 7*.
○ **C.** Glenn became the first American to orbit the Earth.
○ **D.** Glenn flew in space for the first time.

D. Crayons have been around for more than a hundred years. But they have changed a lot.

The first crayons were all black. Workers in shipyards used them to label crates. Then, in the early 1900s, the Crayola company decided to make colorful crayons for kids. The first box had eight colors: black, brown, red, blue, purple, orange, yellow, and green. The box cost just five cents.

Today, there are hundreds of crayon colors, from "tickle me pink" to "tropical rain forest." Scientists keep blending different colors to come up with new shades. Then the scientists show the new color to kids to see if they will use it. Crayon companies have also asked children to help name new crayon colors.

I. This story is mostly about
   ○ **A.** rain forests.
   ○ **B.** scientists.
   ○ **C.** rainbows.
   ○ **D.** crayons.

2. You can guess from the story that
   ○ **A.** a box of crayons costs more than five cents today.
   ○ **B.** crayon companies no longer make plain red crayons.
   ○ **C.** no one uses crayons anymore.
   ○ **D.** "tropical rain forest" is a shade of blue.

3. This story would probably go on to talk about
   ○ **A.** shipyard workers.
   ○ **B.** kids' favorite crayon colors.
   ○ **C.** the history of paper.
   ○ **D.** the first crayons.

E. Respect Them, Protect Them

Splish, splash! Splish, splash!
Fish frolic in the seas.
Swish, swoosh! Swish, swoosh!
Birds fly in the breeze.

Scritch, scratch! Scritch, scratch!
Crabs dig in the sand.
Romp, stomp! Romp, stomp!
Animals roam the land.

Seas, breeze, sand, land.
There are creatures everywhere.
Respect them, **protect** them
On this planet that we share.

By Karen Kellaher

I. In the poem, the word **protect** means
   ○ **A.** keep safe.
   ○ **B.** see.
   ○ **C.** know.
   ○ **D.** dig.

2. You'd probably find this poem in a
   ○ **A.** book of autumn poems.
   ○ **B.** book of animal poems.
   ○ **C.** book of New Year's poems.
   ○ **D.** book of Halloween poems

3. The poet probably wrote the poem
   ○ **A.** to convince kids to study hard in school.
   ○ **B.** to teach people about crabs.
   ○ **C.** to celebrate winter.
   ○ **D.** to convince people to help animals.

VOCABULARY
Which Word Is Missing?

In each of the following paragraphs, a word is missing. First, read the paragraph. Then find the missing word in the list of words beneath the paragraph. Fill in the circle next to the word that is missing.

Sample:

I have a lot of homework, so I should get started on it _____.
- ○ **A.** someday
- ○ **B.** maybe
- ○ **C.** soon
- ○ **D.** later

There was a pie-eating contest at the fair. Jonathan entered the contest and ate four pies. He won first _____.
- ○ **A.** prize
- ○ **B.** day
- ○ **C.** pie
- ○ **D.** stop

1. Icy Antarctica is not an easy place to live. In summer, this continent has an average temperature of zero degrees. In winter, the temperature can drop to 100 degrees below zero! Brrrr! Few creatures can live in such _____ conditions.
- ○ **A.** cold
- ○ **B.** warm
- ○ **C.** strange
- ○ **D.** ugly

2. However, penguins do not seem to mind the cold. These birds live along Antarctica's coast. They spend some of their time on land. But they spend most of their time in the chilly _____ around Antarctica.
- ○ **A.** birds
- ○ **B.** feathers
- ○ **C.** lands
- ○ **D.** waters

3. How do penguins stay warm? They have a thick layer of fat called blubber. And they have oily black and white _____ to keep the icy water away from their skin.
- ○ **A.** windows
- ○ **B.** head
- ○ **C.** feathers
- ○ **D.** eyes

4. Penguins cannot _____ like most birds. Instead, they waddle around on two feet. Sometimes they slide on the ice on their stomachs.
- ○ **A.** read
- ○ **B.** fly
- ○ **C.** eat
- ○ **D.** see

5. In the ocean, penguins can dive _____ under the water. They swim by opening and closing their wings and paddling their feet.
- ○ **A.** never
- ○ **B.** late
- ○ **C.** deep
- ○ **D.** walk

6. Penguins live in groups. Mothers lay their eggs in a spot called a rookery. There can be thousands of penguins in one rookery. Even in the ocean, penguins stick _____.
- ○ **A.** home
- ○ **B.** together
- ○ **C.** alone
- ○ **D.** cousin

7. Penguins don't eat a lot. They usually munch on fish and tiny creatures called krill. When they are very _____, they might eat a squid.
- ○ **A.** hungry
- ○ **B.** tired
- ○ **C.** cold
- ○ **D.** gone

Reading Skills Practice Test 7

READING COMPREHENSION

Read each story. Then fill in the circle that best completes each sentence or answers each question.

SAMPLE

A dolphin is a sea animal. However, it is not a fish and cannot breathe in water. It is a type of whale. It must come up to the **surface** to breathe air. Dolphins travel through the sea in large groups.

1. What is the best title for this story?
   ○ A. "Breathing"
   ○ B. "Fish"
   ○ C. "Dolphins"
   ○ D. "Animals"

2. In this story, the word **surface** means
   ○ A. the top of the water.
   ○ B. the bottom of the sea.
   ○ C. an ocean rock.
   ○ D. a sea plant.

A. Sojourner Truth was born into slavery in New York in 1797. When she was 9 years old, Sojourner's owner separated her from her mother and sold her to another slave owner. Sojourner remained a slave until she was 30. After she was set free, she spent the rest of her life traveling and speaking out against slavery. She even met with President Abraham Lincoln.

1. This story is mainly about
   ○ A. Abraham Lincoln.
   ○ B. slavery.
   ○ C. New York.
   ○ D. Sojourner Truth.

2. You would probably find this story in a book about
   ○ A. New York City.
   ○ B. famous women.
   ○ C. Presidents.
   ○ D. speeches.

3. Which happened first?
   ○ A. Sojourner met Lincoln.
   ○ B. Sojourner was set free.
   ○ C. Sojourner was taken from her mother.
   ○ D. Sojourner spoke out against slavery.

B.   Many people think spiders are creepy. But some scientists say we can learn a lot from these eight-legged creatures. Scientists are studying the sticky strands of silk that spiders use to weave their webs. The silk is very strong. Scientists are trying to make thread in their labs that is just like spider silk, only thicker. They hope this thick "spider silk" can be turned into strong cables that can be used to hold up bridges.

1.   Scientists hope to use thread that is like spider silk to make

    ○ **A.** webs.   ○ **C.** cables.

    ○ **B.** steel.   ○ **D.** rugs.

2.   The author wrote this story to

    ○ **A.** tell a scary story.

    ○ **B.** show the value of spider silk.

    ○ **C.** explain why bridges are strong.

    ○ **D.** tell how cloth is made.

C.   Venus is sometimes called Earth's "sister" or "twin." That's because it is the planet **nearest** to Earth. It's also about the same size as Earth.

    But Venus is different from Earth in many ways. Venus is much hotter than Earth. It is about 850 degrees on Venus's surface! The air, or atmosphere, around Venus is thick and heavy. It's so thick you can't even see through it. This air traps the sun's heat.

1.   What is the best title for this story?

    ○ **A.** "Nine Planets"

    ○ **B.** "Hot Air"

    ○ **C.** "Sisters"

    ○ **D.** "Earth's Hot Twin"

2.   One reason Venus is called Earth's twin is because

    ○ **A.** they are both planets.

    ○ **B.** they are both very hot.

    ○ **C.** they are about the same size.

    ○ **D.** they have the same air.

3.   In this story, the word **nearest** means

    ○ **A.** hottest.

    ○ **B.** closest.

    ○ **C.** driest.

    ○ **D.** roundest.

D.   The way dogs act around human families has a lot to do with how their wild ancestors lived. Wolves and other wild dogs live in groups or packs with one leader. Today, a pet dog still acts as if it lives in a pack. It **behaves** as if its owner is its pack leader. That makes it easy for people to train dogs.

1.   In this story, the word **behaves** means

    ○ **A.** eats.

    ○ **B.** plays.

    ○ **C.** acts.

    ○ **D.** leads.

2.   You can guess from this story that

    ○ **A.** dogs are difficult to train.

    ○ **B.** dogs are related to wolves.

    ○ **C.** all dogs want to be a pack leader.

    ○ **D.** dogs like to live alone.

E.   Each year in Japan, children celebrate *Undokai*, or Sports Day. On this special day, schools compete against each other in relay races and other track events. One favorite race is the *daruma*. In this event, runners race in pairs. One runner in the pair wears something over his or her head, making it impossible to see. This runner is **guided** by his or her partner, who carries a small ball on a scoop. If the ball drops, the pair of runners must start the race over!

I. What is the best title for this story?
- ○ **A.** "Races Through History"
- ○ **B.** "Sports Day in Japan"
- ○ **C.** "Japan Today"
- ○ **D.** "Teams"

2. Who competes on Sports Day?
- ○ **A.** children
- ○ **B.** parents
- ○ **C.** professional athletes
- ○ **D.** teachers

3. In this story, the word **guided** means
- ○ **A.** won.
- ○ **B.** led.
- ○ **C.** followed.
- ○ **D.** driven.

F.   A bike helmet is made of hard foam. The foam absorbs the force of a fall so that the hard ground does not hurt your head. But your helmet won't protect your head if it doesn't fit right. Here are some tips for **selecting** the best helmet.
- Try on helmets at a bike store. Pick one that isn't too tight. But make sure it isn't so big that it rocks back and forth.
- Most helmets come with soft pads. Stick the pads on the inside of the helmet to make it fit just right.
- Keep the front of your helmet just above your eyebrows when you ride.
- Make sure the chin strap fits snugly under your chin. The strap holds the helmet on if you are in an accident.

I. In this story, the word **selecting** means
- ○ **A.** wearing.
- ○ **B.** riding.
- ○ **C.** choosing.
- ○ **D.** cleaning.

2. You can guess from the story that
- ○ **A.** loose helmets might slip off.
- ○ **B.** chin straps often break.
- ○ **C.** it hurts to wear a helmet.
- ○ **D.** bike riding is always safe.

3. Bike helmets are needed because
- ○ **A.** all bike riders go too fast.
- ○ **B.** kids are careless.
- ○ **C.** they protect your head.
- ○ **D.** they keep your head warm.

4. Which of these is an *opinion* about helmets?
- ○ **A.** They are made of hard foam.
- ○ **B.** They must fit correctly.
- ○ **C.** They have chin straps.
- ○ **D.** They are attractive.

VOCABULARY

Synonyms

Read the underlined word in each phrase. Mark the word below it that has the same (or close to the same) meaning.

Sample:

mend the sweater
- ○ **A.** rip
- ○ **B.** raise
- ○ **C.** wear
- ○ **D.** fix

1. discover treasure
   - ○ **A.** bury
   - ○ **B.** find
   - ○ **C.** golden
   - ○ **D.** pirate

2. false alarm
   - ○ **A.** loud
   - ○ **B.** long
   - ○ **C.** mistaken
   - ○ **D.** true

3. receive a gift
   - ○ **A.** get
   - ○ **B.** give
   - ○ **C.** lose
   - ○ **D.** wrap

4. old custom
   - ○ **A.** trunk
   - ○ **B.** clothes
   - ○ **C.** money
   - ○ **D.** tradition

5. long silence
   - ○ **A.** quiet
   - ○ **B.** storm
   - ○ **C.** light
   - ○ **D.** package

6. complete the test
   - ○ **A.** finish
   - ○ **B.** fail
   - ○ **C.** lose
   - ○ **D.** write

7. scent of roses
   - ○ **A.** field
   - ○ **B.** store
   - ○ **C.** color
   - ○ **D.** smell

Multiple Meanings

Read each set of sentences. Mark the word that makes sense in both sentences.

Sample:

The doctor put the girl's broken leg in a _____.
The _____ of that TV show is very talented.
- ○ **A.** cast
- ○ **B.** sling
- ○ **C.** actor
- ○ **D.** station

1. Can you help me _____ a shirt?
   The machine is made of _____.
   - ○ **A.** steel
   - ○ **B.** wash
   - ○ **C.** iron
   - ○ **D.** find

2. I would love another _____ of stew.
   He is known for _____ others.
   - ○ **A.** share
   - ○ **B.** plate
   - ○ **C.** teaching
   - ○ **D.** helping

3. Mom wrote a _____ to pay for the groceries.
   The teacher wants us to _____ our homework.
   - ○ **A.** check
   - ○ **B.** do
   - ○ **C.** bill
   - ○ **D.** note

4. There is a _____ on your shirt.
   If you _____ a parking space, let me know.
   - ○ **A.** stain
   - ○ **B.** spot
   - ○ **C.** see
   - ○ **D.** button

Reading Skills Practice Test 8

READING COMPREHENSION

Read each story. Then fill in the circle that best completes each sentence or answers each question.

Mars is called the "Red Planet." That's because the **soil** on Mars has a lot of rust. Rust is the same substance that forms on a bicycle left out in the rain. The rusty dirt makes Mars look red.

I. The best title for this story is
    ○ **A.** "Mars: The Orange Planet."
    ○ **B.** "Mars: The Red Planet."
    ○ **C.** "Take Care of Your Bike."
    ○ **D.** "Plants on Mars."

2. In the story, the word **soil** means
    ○ **A.** air.
    ○ **B.** bike.
    ○ **C.** dirt.
    ○ **D.** red.

A. Imagine a music group that has no guitars, pianos, or drums. Instead, its members make music with brooms, trash cans, and pot lids!

Believe it or not, this **odd** group really exists. It is called *Stomp. Stomp* started in England in 1991. Since then, it has performed all over the world. It is famous for its lively music and funny shows.

I. The best title for this story is
    ○ **A.** "Playing the Piano."
    ○ **B.** "The History of Music."
    ○ **C.** "*Stomp*'s Unusual Music."
    ○ **D.** "English Musicians."

2. The members of *Stomp* play
    ○ **A.** guitars.   ○ **C.** flutes.
    ○ **B.** trash cans.   ○ **D.** pianos.

3. In the story, the word **odd** means
    ○ **A.** helpful.
    ○ **B.** lost.
    ○ **C.** old.
    ○ **D.** unusual.

4. You would probably find this story
    ○ **A.** in a magazine about music.
    ○ **B.** in a history book.
    ○ **C.** in a book about pianos.
    ○ **D.** in a geography book.

5. Which of these is an *opinion*?
    ○ **A.** *Stomp* started in England.
    ○ **B.** *Stomp*'s music is too loud.
    ○ **C.** *Stomp* does not use drums.
    ○ **D.** *Stomp* began in 1991.

B. In the 1800s, American women were not allowed to vote. Many people fought to change that. They were called *suffragists*.

One famous suffragist was Elizabeth Cady Stanton. In 1848, she planned a meeting called the Seneca Falls Convention. More than 100 people met to talk about women's rights. Stanton **spoke** to them. She said that "men and women are created equal."

In 1878, lawmakers finally listened to Stanton and the other suffragists. They started talking about changing the law to give women the right to vote. The law finally changed 42 years later.

I. This story is mainly about
○ **A.** Susan B. Anthony.
○ **B.** Elizabeth Cady Stanton.
○ **C.** the history of the United States.
○ **D.** many famous women.

2. The Seneca Falls Convention was in
○ **A.** 1800.   ○ **C.** 1848.
○ **B.** 1828.   ○ **D.** 1878.

3. In the story, the word **spoke** means
○ **A.** talked.
○ **B.** found.
○ **C.** a part of a wheel.
○ **D.** helped.

4. You can guess from this story that
○ **A.** Stanton didn't think men should have the right to vote.
○ **B.** Stanton was very rich.
○ **C.** American women can vote today.
○ **D.** lawmakers did not like Stanton.

C. Do you love to ride on a racing roller coaster? You are not alone. Roller coasters have been thrilling riders for hundreds of years!

Roller coasters got their start in Russia 600 years ago. Back then, there were no lightning-fast loops. Instead, riders just slid down icy mountains. By 1700, people were making rides that used tracks and wheels instead of ice.

The first American coaster was built in Coney Island, New York, in 1884. It was the Switchback Railway. It looked like a train going down a mountain. Soon, other parks made similar rides, and roller coasters really took off!

I. The first American roller coaster was called the
○ **A.** Loop-A-Rama.
○ **B.** Coney Island.
○ **C.** Superdrop.
○ **D.** Switchback Railway.

2. Which of these happened *first*?
○ **A.** An American coaster was built.
○ **B.** Russian people slid down icy mountains.
○ **C.** Coasters started using wheels.
○ **D.** The Switchback Railway opened.

3. The story would probably go on to talk about
○ **A.** today's roller coasters.
○ **B.** weather in Russia.
○ **C.** where Coney Island is located.
○ **D.** railroads of the world.

D.   Most people have never heard of Patty Smith Hill. But almost everyone knows this songwriter's famous work!

Patty Smith Hill was a teacher who lived in Kentucky more than 100 years ago. In 1893, she was **searching** for songs for children to sing at school. She decided to write one of her own. She wrote words to a song and called it "Good Morning to All." Smith's sister, Mildred, wrote some music to go with the words.

Schoolchildren loved the sisters' song. In 1924, the Smiths added a new verse to the song. It was called, "Happy Birthday to You." Sound familiar? It's now one of the most famous songs in the world!

1. This story is mostly about
   ○ **A.** the history of a popular song.
   ○ **B.** children around the world.
   ○ **C.** living in Kentucky.
   ○ **D.** how people can work together.

2. Patty Smith Hill wrote the "Happy Birthday" song with her
   ○ **A.** father.   ○ **C.** brother.
   ○ **B.** mother.   ○ **D.** sister.

3. In the story, the word **searching** means
   ○ **A.** singing.   ○ **C.** driving.
   ○ **B.** looking.   ○ **D.** knowing.

4. The author probably wrote the story
   ○ **A.** to get readers to sing.
   ○ **B.** to celebrate his or her birthday.
   ○ **C.** to make Patty Smith Hill happy.
   ○ **D.** to give readers some history.

E.   For six states in the middle of our country, springtime brings more than birds and flowers. It also brings tornadoes.

Tornadoes, or twisters, can strike almost anywhere. But many tornadoes happen in Texas, Oklahoma, Kansas, Nebraska, Iowa, and Missouri. These states are called "Tornado Alley."

A tornado is a spinning column of air that forms in the middle of a thunderstorm. Inside a tornado, air spins at nearly 300 miles per hour. The spinning air acts like a vacuum. It can pull trees from the ground and make cars fly through the sky.

The United States has hundreds of tornadoes every year. Luckily, only a few of them are strong enough to cause damage.

1. You can guess from the story that
   ○ **A.** most tornadoes happen in fall.
   ○ **B.** "twister" is another word for tornado.
   ○ **C.** Iowa gets more tornadoes than Kansas does.
   ○ **D.** Missouri does not get tornadoes.

2. A tornado's spinning air can cause
   ○ **A.** thunderstorms to begin.
   ○ **B.** flowers to bloom.
   ○ **C.** springtime to start early.
   ○ **D.** cars to fly through the sky.

3. Which of these is a *fact* about tornadoes?
   ○ **A.** They are scarier than blizzards.
   ○ **B.** They are interesting to study.
   ○ **C.** They often happen in spring.
   ○ **D.** They should be called "spinners."

VOCABULARY

Synonyms
Read the underlined word in each phrase. Mark the word below it that has the same (or close to the same) meaning.

Sample:

a huge <u>feast</u>
- ○ **A.** letter
- ○ **B.** wish
- ○ **C.** lawn
- ○ **D.** meal

1. <u>frighten</u> him
   - ○ **A.** ask
   - ○ **B.** scare
   - ○ **C.** draw
   - ○ **D.** pull

2. a long <u>battle</u>
   - ○ **A.** year
   - ○ **B.** bag
   - ○ **C.** fight
   - ○ **D.** nail

3. a fire <u>blazed</u>
   - ○ **A.** cleaned
   - ○ **B.** stopped
   - ○ **C.** fell
   - ○ **D.** burned

4. a feeling of <u>joy</u>
   - ○ **A.** fear
   - ○ **B.** happiness
   - ○ **C.** anger
   - ○ **D.** sadness

5. don't <u>disturb</u> her
   - ○ **A.** bother
   - ○ **B.** let
   - ○ **C.** smile
   - ○ **D.** grow

6. <u>calm</u> sea
   - ○ **A.** peaceful
   - ○ **B.** my
   - ○ **C.** far
   - ○ **D.** locked

7. famous <u>author</u>
   - ○ **A.** meal
   - ○ **B.** driver
   - ○ **C.** eat
   - ○ **D.** writer

8. he <u>declared</u>
   - ○ **A.** dreamed
   - ○ **B.** truck
   - ○ **C.** said
   - ○ **D.** moved

Multiple Meanings
Read each set of sentences. Mark the word that makes sense in both sentences.

Sample:

Margaret is a stylish _____.
I have a new _____ in my bedroom.
- ○ **A.** painting
- ○ **B.** bed
- ○ **C.** dresser
- ○ **D.** door

1. I was so hungry, I felt like I might _____.
   We could see very _____ numbers on the old mailbox.
   - ○ **A.** starve
   - ○ **B.** faint
   - ○ **C.** low
   - ○ **D.** many

2. I _____ my spelling book at school.
   Gregory writes with his _____ hand.
   - ○ **A.** right
   - ○ **B.** leave
   - ○ **C.** bought
   - ○ **D.** left

3. My neighbor asked me to _____ her dog while she's on vacation.
   Katie looked like something was on her _____.
   - ○ **A.** shirt
   - ○ **B.** mind
   - ○ **C.** keep
   - ○ **D.** feed

4. I like steak cooked until it is well done, but my brother likes it _____.
   That rain forest bird is very _____.
   - ○ **A.** burned
   - ○ **B.** colorful
   - ○ **C.** beautiful
   - ○ **D.** rare

5. The runners jog around the _____.
   Our teacher told us to keep _____ of how much we read each night.
   - ○ **A.** school
   - ○ **B.** records
   - ○ **C.** track
   - ○ **D.** street

Reading Skills Practice Test 9

READING COMPREHENSION

Read each story. Then fill in the circle that best completes each sentence or answers each question.

What does your last name say about you? If you lived in England in the 1100s, it told others what you did for a living. For example, people in the Parker family were park keepers, and the Baker **clan** actually baked bread and cakes! The Walls were builders, while the Smiths were blacksmiths. If your family's name is one of these, you may have a clue about how your ancestors earned a living!

1. What is the best title for this story?
   - ○ **A.** "Make a Family Tree"
   - ○ **B.** "Names Tell Stories"
   - ○ **C.** "How to Choose a Job"
   - ○ **D.** "Builders of Long Ago"

2. In this story, the word **clan** means
   - ○ **A.** time.
   - ○ **B.** clue.
   - ○ **C.** family.
   - ○ **D.** bread.

A. Here's some good news for pizza lovers! Pizza is not just tasty, it also provides important nutrients your body needs. Tomatoes, cheese, and wheat crust all contain vitamins to keep your body healthy and strong. Add some mushrooms or peppers on top, and you'll pack in even more vitamins. Pizza cheese has protein, which your body uses to grow and **repair** cells. Pizza dough has plenty of carbohydrates—the nutrients that give you energy to play and learn. And, last but not least, the cheese and oil on pizza have fats, which your body needs to store energy over time. Of course, too much fat is bad for your heart, so it's smart to save pizza for a special treat.

1. This story is mainly about
   - ○ **A.** ways to serve pizza.
   - ○ **B.** kids' favorite pizza toppings.
   - ○ **C.** the invention of pizza.
   - ○ **D.** the nutrients in pizza.

2. In this story, the word **repair** means
   - ○ **A.** fix.   ○ **C.** eat.
   - ○ **B.** lose.   ○ **D.** cook.

3. Cheese and oil both contain
   - ○ **A.** protein.   ○ **C.** pizza.
   - ○ **B.** fat.   ○ **D.** carbohydrates.

4. You can guess from the story that
   - ○ **A.** you should never eat pizza.
   - ○ **B.** you should not eat pizza every day.
   - ○ **C.** pizza is very hard to make.
   - ○ **D.** pizza has 20 different ingredients.

B. In dinosaur movies and TV shows, dinos hiss, hoot, screech, and roar. But in real life, paleontologists, or dinosaur experts, don't know what kinds of sounds dinosaurs made. These experts do believe that dinosaurs made some type of noise, however. And they can make some guesses based on studies of dinosaur skulls. For example, paleontologists say that many dinos had pointy crests on their heads. These hollow crests would have filled with air when the dinosaur breathed. As air moved through the crest, the dinosaur probably made a deep bellowing or roaring sound.

Experts also say that dinosaurs probably had good reasons to make noise. Like other creatures, dinos probably made sounds to warn fellow dinosaurs away from danger, to find mates, and to communicate with their young.

l. This story is mainly about
- ○ **A.** how paleontologists work.
- ○ **B.** dinosaur skeletons.
- ○ **C.** how dinosaurs breathed.
- ○ **D.** the noises dinosaurs made.

2. According to the story, which of these is probably *not* a reason for dinosaurs to have made noise?
- ○ **A.** to warn fellow dinos from danger
- ○ **B.** to find mates
- ○ **C.** to entertain each other
- ○ **D.** to communicate with their young

3. Air moving through a dinosaur's crest would have caused
- ○ **A.** a deep bellowing noise.
- ○ **B.** a low rumbling noise.
- ○ **C.** hisses, hoots, and screeches.
- ○ **D.** breathing problems.

4. Which of these is a *fact* about dinosaurs?
- ○ **A.** Dinosaurs made frightening sounds.
- ○ **B.** Many dinosaurs had crests.
- ○ **C.** Dinosaurs are dull.
- ○ **D.** Dinosaurs are interesting.

C. If you like talking to people and writing stories, being a news reporter may be the job for you. It is challenging, though! Reporters work hard and face tough deadlines. They follow four steps to finish a news story:

1. Do research. When reporters learn about a news event, they gather facts. They **interview** people involved in the event and take careful notes. They try to answer the questions *who, what, when, where, why,* and *how.*

2. Write the lead. The lead of a news story is the first sentence or several sentences. The lead tells the most important idea of the story and makes the reader want to keep reading.

3. Write the body of the story. The body, or main part, of the story, gives details that support the lead sentence. Sometimes, the body contains quotes from the people interviewed by the reporter.

4. Write a headline. A headline is the title of a news story. It should summarize the main idea of the story and grab the reader's attention.

l. What is the best title for this story?
- ○ **A.** "This Week's Top News"
- ○ **B.** "How Reporters Write Stories"
- ○ **C.** "Writing Good Headlines"
- ○ **D.** "The Research Process"

2. In this story the word **interview** means
- ○ **A.** talk to.   ○ **C.** share.
- ○ **B.** read to.   ○ **D.** summarize.

3. To write a news story, what should you do first?
- ○ **A.** Write the body.
- ○ **B.** Write the lead.
- ○ **C.** Write the headline.
- ○ **D.** Do research.

4. The first sentence or sentences of a news story is called the
- ○ **A.** body.   ○ **C.** lead.
- ○ **B.** interview.   ○ **D.** caption.

D.
The Robin
A Mother Goose Rhyme

The north wind doth blow,
And we **shall** have snow,
And what will the robin do then,
                    Poor thing?

He'll sit in a barn,
And keep himself warm,
And hide his head under his wing,
                    Poor thing!

I. Another good title for this poem
might be
○ **A.** "A Robin's Nest."
○ **B.** "A Robin in Winter."
○ **C.** "The North Wind."
○ **D.** "Snow Is on the Way."

2. In this poem, the word **shall** means
○ **A.** flies.
○ **B.** hope.
○ **C.** will.
○ **D.** did.

3. The poet probably created this rhyme to
○ **A.** entertain people.
○ **B.** entertain robins.
○ **C.** explain snowfall.
○ **D.** celebrate springtime.

4. You can guess from the poem that
○ **A.** robins only live where it's cold.
○ **B.** robins enjoy cold weather.
○ **C.** the poet feels sorry for robins.
○ **D.** the poet dislikes robins.

E.

Loch Ness is a lake in northern Scotland. It is also home to a famous story—the **legend** of the Loch Ness Monster.

The legend began 1,500 years ago. That's when people near the lake first began talking about a strange sea beast. Then, in 1933, a couple said they saw a giant creature tossing and turning in the lake. Newspapers all over the world reported the strange event.

Since then, about 4,000 people have claimed to see the creature in the lake. They have even given it a name—Nessie. Some people say they saw Nessie's huge head. Others say they saw its neck or tail. But no one has ever been able to prove that the creature really exists.

In 1987, scientists wanted to find out if there was truth behind the legend. They used special equipment to search for living things in the lake. They found a lot of salmon and other fish, but no monster.

I. In this story, the word **legend** means
○ **A.** country.
○ **B.** creature.
○ **C.** lake.
○ **D.** story.

2. The best title for this story is
○ **A.** "Lakes of Scotland."
○ **B.** "The Legend of Nessie."
○ **C.** "Monster Stories."
○ **D.** "Scientists Find Loch Ness Monster."

3. You can guess from the story that
○ **A.** the Loch Ness Monster is red.
○ **B.** Scotland has only one lake.
○ **C.** many people don't believe in the Loch Ness Monster.
○ **D.** there really is a monster in the lake.

VOCABULARY

Synonyms

Read the underlined word in each phrase. Mark the word below it that has the same (or close to the same) meaning.

Sample:

glance over
- ○ **A.** look
- ○ **B.** try
- ○ **C.** return
- ○ **D.** share

1. the calm ocean
   - ○ **A.** cold
   - ○ **B.** deep
   - ○ **C.** rough
   - ○ **D.** peaceful

2. the final game
   - ○ **A.** hardest
   - ○ **B.** last
   - ○ **C.** first
   - ○ **D.** best

3. stumble over it
   - ○ **A.** trip
   - ○ **B.** fight
   - ○ **C.** hear
   - ○ **D.** leap

4. a timid boy
   - ○ **A.** intelligent
   - ○ **B.** tired
   - ○ **C.** shy
   - ○ **D.** happy

5. reply quickly
   - ○ **A.** pull
   - ○ **B.** answer
   - ○ **C.** draw
   - ○ **D.** lock

6. twist the top
   - ○ **A.** touch
   - ○ **B.** turn
   - ○ **C.** close
   - ○ **D.** lift

7. trembling like a leaf
   - ○ **A.** falling
   - ○ **B.** shaking
   - ○ **C.** growing
   - ○ **D.** living

Multiple Meanings

Read each set of sentences. Mark the word that makes sense in both sentences.

Sample:

George lost his new _____ at the park.
I want to _____ the sun set tonight.
- ○ **A.** book
- ○ **B.** watch
- ○ **C.** see
- ○ **D.** pen

1. The kids lined up in alphabetical _____ .

   "May I take your _____?" he asked.
   - ○ **A.** line
   - ○ **B.** coat
   - ○ **C.** name
   - ○ **D.** order

2. Hillary threw the ball with all her _____ .

   The Joneses _____ stop by for a visit.
   - ○ **A.** strength
   - ○ **B.** did
   - ○ **C.** might
   - ○ **D.** may

3. _____ blew air around the room.
   The team's _____ applauded every play.
   - ○ **A.** fans
   - ○ **B.** wind
   - ○ **C.** coach
   - ○ **D.** they

4. All people have a _____ to food and shelter.
   Do you know the _____ answer?
   - ○ **A.** next
   - ○ **B.** right
   - ○ **C.** need
   - ○ **D.** best

5. The man helped his mother _____ the bus.
   The students made a bulletin _____ for winter.
   - ○ **A.** board
   - ○ **B.** ride
   - ○ **C.** catch
   - ○ **D.** poster

Reading Skills Practice Test 10

READING COMPREHENSION

Read each story. Then fill in the circle that best completes each sentence or answers each question.

SAMPLE

Is your smile full of holes these days? You are not alone. Most kids your age are losing their baby teeth. Baby teeth fall out to make room for permanent teeth. Baby teeth fall out when their roots **shrink**. The roots are what hold the teeth in the jawbone.

I. The best title for this story is
○ A. "Goodbye, Baby Teeth."
○ B. "How Cavities Form."
○ C. "How to Care for Teeth."
○ D. "The Tooth Fairy."

2. In the story, the word **shrink** means
○ A. grow.
○ B. get sick.
○ C. get smaller.
○ D. appear.

A. Before money was invented, people **exchanged** one kind of goods for another. For example, long ago, people used shells, beans, or beads to buy food. Later, people began to make coins out of valuable materials like silver and gold.

Today, we use paper money and coins to buy things. Our money is not made of precious materials, but it is valuable all the same. Each bill or coin is worth the amount printed or stamped on it.

I. The best title for this story is
○ A. "How to Make Money."
○ B. "The History of Money."
○ C. "Rare Coins."
○ D. "Working at a Bank."

2. What do we use for money today?
○ A. gold   ○ C. bills and coins
○ B. shells   ○ D. beans and beads

3. In the story, the word **exchanged** means
○ A. helped.   ○ C. lost.
○ B. traded.   ○ D. made.

4. Which of these happened first?
○ A. Silver coins were invented.
○ B. Gold coins were invented.
○ C. Paper money was invented.
○ D. People used beads to buy food.

5. You can guess from the story that
○ A. beads have been around a long time.
○ B. people have always used paper money.
○ C. money was invented in the U.S.
○ D. shells are more valuable than coins.

B.   On January 20, 1951, a snowstorm hit the village of Andermatt, Switzerland. For many hours, snow fell on the village and the tall mountains nearby.

Suddenly, around 2 p.m., a giant slab of snow rolled down a mountain onto Andermatt. It was an avalanche. Within hours, three more avalanches fell on the village. The avalanches crushed homes and buried the village's main street.

Rescuers worked quickly to help the villagers. Rescue dogs helped too. They used their strong noses to sniff out people who were **trapped** in the snow.

I.   This story is mainly about
○ **A.** Europe.
○ **B.** snowstorms.
○ **C.** dogs.
○ **D.** avalanches in a village in Switzerland.

2.   How many avalanches fell on Andermatt on January 20, 1951?
○ **A.** one   ○ **C.** three
○ **B.** two   ○ **D.** four

3.   In the story, the word **trapped** means
○ **A.** stuck.   ○ **C.** sniffed.
○ **B.** playing.   ○ **D.** helped.

4.   Which sentence is an *opinion* about avalanches?
○ **A.** They can happen suddenly.
○ **B.** They are the worst kinds of disaster.
○ **C.** They can crush a village.
○ **D.** They happen when snow falls down a mountain.

C.   Hundreds of years ago, grasslands called prairies covered the middle part of the United States. The prairie land stretched from southern Canada to northern Mexico. Prairie dogs, buffalo, and other animals roamed the prairie and ate the wild grasses.

In the 1800s, the number of people in our country began to grow. All those people needed somewhere to live. Many of them built homes and farms where the prairie used to be. Most of the prairie disappeared.

Today, some people are working to bring back pieces of the prairie. First, they find a piece of land that used to be a prairie. Then they plant prairie grass seeds and wait patiently for the wild grass to come back.

I.   One example of a prairie animal is a
○ **A.** buffalo.   ○ **B.** bear.
○ **C.** monkey.   ○ **D.** squirrel.

2.   The best title for this passage is
○ **A.** "Prairie Animals."
○ **B.** "Prairies: Then and Now."
○ **C.** "Where to Find Prairie Grass."
○ **D.** "Growth of Our Country."

3.   The prairies disappeared because
○ **A.** people built homes and farms.
○ **B.** prairie dogs ate all the grass.
○ **C.** the prairie grasses all died.
○ **D.** Canada took over the prairie land.

4.   You can guess from the story that
○ **A.** the prairie used to be very large.
○ **B.** there are no more prairie dogs.
○ **C.** prairie grass is ugly.
○ **D.** prairie land turned into forest land.

D.   For a hundred years, people have told the tale of John Henry, one of the strongest men who ever lived.

According to **legend**, John Henry was born with a hammer in his hand. When John Henry grew up, he took a job with the railroad. He used his hammer to chip away mountains so the train tracks could pass through.

One day, a man with a fancy new drilling machine challenged John Henry to a contest. For nine hours, both men would chip away at the mountain. The man who carved farther into the mountain would be the winner.

As John Henry worked, sweat poured from his body. But his strong arms kept hammering. Finally, a judge measured how far each man had gone. John Henry won. With his simple hammer, he had chipped away 20 feet of rock—and beat a fancy machine!

I.   What tool did John Henry use?
   ○ **A.** a hammer   ○ **C.** a drill
   ○ **B.** a saw   ○ **D.** a tractor

2.   In the story, the word **legend** means
   ○ **A.** a story handed down from long ago.
   ○ **B.** a special kind of hammer.
   ○ **C.** a mountain made of rock.
   ○ **D.** a strong person.

3.   Which of these did John Henry do last?
   ○ **A.** He joined a contest.
   ○ **B.** He was born.
   ○ **C.** He chipped away 20 feet of rock.
   ○ **D.** He got a job with the railroad.

4.   Next, the story would probably talk about
   ○ **A.** John Henry's mom and dad.
   ○ **B.** John Henry's next adventure.
   ○ **C.** how to build a railroad.
   ○ **D.** other types of hammers.

E.   Guide dogs are a big help to blind people. A guide dog helps its owner cross the street and do many other things. But it is not easy to become a guide dog. Here's what a dog must do to get the job:

1. When the dog is a puppy, trainers watch the dog to make sure it is friendly and calm.
2. For one year, the dog goes to live with a family. The family teaches the dog some **simple** commands, like "Sit!" and "Stay!"
3. Then the dog goes to school, where trainers teach the dog to lead a person. The dog must learn to steer clear of cars and other dangers.
4. The trainers take the dog into town to practice going into stores and banks.
5. If the dog has done well at school, it is ready to meet its blind owner. Now they will work as a team.

I.   In this story, the word **simple** means
   ○ **A.** easy.   ○ **C.** hidden.
   ○ **B.** happy.   ○ **D.** loving.

2.   You would probably find this story in
   ○ **A.** a book about families.
   ○ **B.** a book of folktales.
   ○ **C.** a book about working animals.
   ○ **D.** a travel book.

3.   This story was probably created to
   ○ **A.** explain how guide dogs are trained.
   ○ **B.** tell people to get pet dogs.
   ○ **C.** compare dogs to other pets.
   ○ **D.** help blind people find the right pet.

4.   Which of these is a *fact* from the story?
   ○ **A.** It is fun to train a dog.
   ○ **B.** Dogs are cute.
   ○ **C.** Guide dogs must be calm.
   ○ **D.** All dogs should be guide dogs.

VOCABULARY

Synonyms

Read the underlined word in each phrase. Mark the word below it that has the same (or close to the same) meaning.

Sample:

receive the package
- ○ **A.** send
- ○ **B.** get
- ○ **C.** paint
- ○ **D.** file

1. create art
   - ○ **A.** make
   - ○ **B.** buy
   - ○ **C.** learn
   - ○ **D.** sight

2. stomachache
   - ○ **A.** order
   - ○ **B.** pill
   - ○ **C.** belly
   - ○ **D.** pain

3. imaginary place
   - ○ **A.** school
   - ○ **B.** pretend
   - ○ **C.** sad
   - ○ **D.** nice

4. a beautiful area
   - ○ **A.** place
   - ○ **B.** person
   - ○ **C.** store
   - ○ **D.** song

5. beneath the desk
   - ○ **A.** sit
   - ○ **B.** under
   - ○ **C.** use
   - ○ **D.** over

6. cellar door
   - ○ **A.** attic
   - ○ **B.** knob
   - ○ **C.** open
   - ○ **D.** basement

7. delicious feast
   - ○ **A.** meal
   - ○ **B.** time
   - ○ **C.** eat
   - ○ **D.** great

8. a long battle
   - ○ **A.** bell
   - ○ **B.** day
   - ○ **C.** fight
   - ○ **D.** jail

Multiple Meanings

Read each set of sentences. Mark the word that makes sense in both sentences.

Sample:

I have a complete _____ of sports cards.
My dad asked me to _____ the table.
- ○ **A.** move
- ○ **B.** set
- ○ **C.** box
- ○ **D.** collection

1. The crossing _____ helps me across the street.
   Will you _____ my bike while I run into the library?
   - ○ **A.** ride
   - ○ **B.** watch
   - ○ **C.** light
   - ○ **D.** guard

2. I can't _____ to put this book down.
   We saw a _____ running in the woods.
   - ○ **A.** deer
   - ○ **B.** man
   - ○ **C.** bear
   - ○ **D.** stand

3. Let's _____ the listings for a movie.
   Ask your mom to write a _____ for your soccer uniform.
   - ○ **A.** read
   - ○ **B.** check
   - ○ **C.** look
   - ○ **D.** letter

4. It's hot, so we turned on the _____.
   I am a big basketball _____.
   - ○ **A.** fan
   - ○ **B.** air
   - ○ **C.** cold
   - ○ **D.** player

5. The teacher asked the class to _____ a straight line.
   Write your name on the _____.
   - ○ **A.** run
   - ○ **B.** blank
   - ○ **C.** form
   - ○ **D.** paper

Reading Skills Practice Test II

READING COMPREHENSION

Read each story. Then fill in the circle that best completes each sentence or answers each question.

Octopuses live in the world's warm oceans. Their bodies are soft and boneless, but they have tough skin called a **mantle** to protect them. Octopuses have eight arms. Their arms are called tentacles. They use their tentacles to catch lobsters, shrimps, clams, and crabs.

I. What is the best title for this story?
 ○ **A.** "Life Under the Sea"
 ○ **B.** "What Fish Eat for Dinner"
 ○ **C.** "The Octopus"
 ○ **D.** "How to Catch a Lobster"

2. In this story, the word **mantle** means
 ○ **A.** tough skin.
 ○ **B.** tentacle.
 ○ **C.** boneless.
 ○ **D.** arm.

A.   There are five steps to writing a story. The first step is called pre-writing. That's when you choose a subject and learn all you can about it. The next step is to write a rough draft of your story. It does not have to be perfect. Then you revise your draft. That means you find ways to make it better. Now you are ready for the fourth step, editing. To edit a story, you correct any mistakes. Finally, you publish, or share, your story. You might read the story aloud or give it to a friend.

I. What is the best title for this story?
 ○ **A.** "My Favorite Subject"
 ○ **B.** "Read to a Friend"
 ○ **C.** "How to Write a Story"
 ○ **D.** "How to Write a Letter"

2. What should you do first?
 ○ **A.** Write a rough draft.
 ○ **B.** Choose a subject.
 ○ **C.** Publish your story.
 ○ **D.** Look for mistakes.

3. To publish a story, you
 ○ **A.** share it with others.
 ○ **B.** collect information.
 ○ **C.** write a rough draft.
 ○ **D.** edit it.

4. You can guess from this story that
 ○ **A.** rough drafts must be perfect.
 ○ **B.** all stories have lots of spelling mistakes.
 ○ **C.** even kids can publish stories.
 ○ **D.** only grown-ups can publish stories.

B. When the Earth travels in its **orbit** around the Sun, it takes 365 $\frac{1}{4}$ calendar days to make the trip. But it would be strange to see $\frac{1}{4}$ of a day on your calendar! So, for three years we save up that $\frac{1}{4}$ day. By the fourth year, it adds up to a whole day! Then we add that extra day to the month of February. When February has 29 days instead of 28, we call that a "leap year."

I. This article is mainly about
○ **A.** why we have leap year.
○ **B.** the seasons of the year.
○ **C.** who invented the calendar.
○ **D.** why February is cold.

2. The Earth travels around the Sun in
○ **A.** 365 days.   ○ **C.** 365 $\frac{1}{4}$ days.
○ **B.** 366 days.   ○ **D.** 366 $\frac{1}{4}$ days.

3. In this article, the word **orbit** means
○ **A.** ship.   ○ **C.** quickly.
○ **B.** path.   ○ **D.** slowly.

4. Which of the following is an *opinion* about February 29?
○ **A.** It comes once every four years.
○ **B.** It's a special day.
○ **C.** It comes during a leap year.
○ **D.** It follows February 28.

C. Digging through old garbage probably doesn't sound fun to you. But that's exactly what a "garbologist" does. A garbologist goes to landfills, where trash is buried. The garbologist digs up the trash to find out how long different things take to decompose, or break down into soil. He or she also looks to see what kinds of trash people throw away.

Why do garbologists care so much about other people's trash? They know that too much garbage is bad for the earth. They want to teach people how to **create** less trash.

I. What is the main idea of this article?
○ **A.** It's not fun to dig through garbage.
○ **B.** "Garbologist" is a silly job name.
○ **C.** Garbologists study garbage to teach people how to make less trash.
○ **D.** Trash is taken to landfills.

2. A landfill is a place where people
○ **A.** live.
○ **B.** bury trash.
○ **C.** recycle trash.
○ **D.** grow food.

3. In this story the word **create** means
○ **A.** make.
○ **B.** dig up.
○ **C.** break down.
○ **D.** decompose.

4. Garbologists dig up trash to
○ **A.** look for buried treasure.
○ **B.** find objects they can sell.
○ **C.** see what kind of trash is there and how long it takes to decompose.
○ **D.** spy on people.

5. You can guess from this story that
○ **A.** garbologists earn a lot of money.
○ **B.** most trash is made of plastic.
○ **C.** landfills can never get too big.
○ **D.** people throw away a lot of garbage.

D.   Anansi the spider thought that if he had a jar full of wisdom, he would be wiser than everybody else. So he walked through his village with a jar, asking the wisest people he knew to put some wisdom in it.

When the jar was full, Anansi decided to hide the jar high up in a tree. He tied a belt around his middle and tucked the jar in front. Then he tried to climb the tree, but the jar kept getting in his way.

Just then Anansi's baby son came along. "Father," he asked, "shouldn't you tuck the jar in the back of the belt?"

Anansi was annoyed. He had a jar full of wisdom, but even a baby was wiser than he was. So after he climbed to the top of the tree, he threw the jar down and smashed it. The wisdom scattered all over the earth. And that is how people got wisdom.

1. The author told this story to tell
- ○ **A.** a few facts about spiders.
- ○ **B.** how people got wisdom.
- ○ **C.** why jars are good for holding things.
- ○ **D.** how people can become smarter.

2. Which happened last?
- ○ **A.** Anansi smashed the jar.
- ○ **B.** Anansi collected wisdom in a jar.
- ○ **C.** Anansi tucked the jar behind him.
- ○ **D.** Anansi climbed the tree.

3. You would probably find this story in
- ○ **A.** a book about spiders.
- ○ **B.** a book about the brain.
- ○ **C.** a book of folktales.
- ○ **D.** a nature guide.

E.   If you think that computers don't belong on a farm, think again! Over the past few years, people have found new ways to make work faster and easier on farms. Here are some of their ideas:
- Farmers need to know how much their animals eat. If the animals don't get enough to eat, they won't be healthy. Now, a farmer can put a special collar on each animal. The collar hooks up to a computer that will **alert** the farmer if the animal is not eating enough.
- It can take dairy farmers hours to milk their cows. But a Dutch company has invented a robot that does all the work. When a cow is ready to be milked, it stands next to the robot. A gate closes, and the robot does the milking.

1. In this story, the word **alert** means
- ○ **A.** warn.   ○ **C.** shout.
- ○ **B.** hide.   ○ **D.** ignore.

2. This story would probably go on to talk about
- ○ **A.** farm animals in different countries.
- ○ **B.** more inventions to help farmers.
- ○ **C.** how to milk a cow by hand.
- ○ **D.** what cows eat.

3. What is the main idea of this story?
- ○ **A.** Milking cows is hard work.
- ○ **B.** Computers don't belong on a farm.
- ○ **C.** Inventions make farm work easier.
- ○ **D.** Farm animals eat a lot.

4. Which is a *fact*?
- ○ **A.** Every farmer in America should have a computer.
- ○ **B.** Cows can be milked by robots.
- ○ **C.** Farmers love new inventions.
- ○ **D.** People are better than robots at milking cows.

VOCABULARY

Synonyms

Read the underlined word in each phrase. Mark the word below it that has the same (or close to the same) meaning.

Sample:

creep across the floor
- ○ **A.** far
- ○ **B.** sneak
- ○ **C.** run
- ○ **D.** stomp

1. burst the bubble
   - ○ **A.** blow
   - ○ **B.** float
   - ○ **C.** soap
   - ○ **D.** pop

2. a loud giggle
   - ○ **A.** sob
   - ○ **B.** sneeze
   - ○ **C.** noise
   - ○ **D.** laugh

3. my favorite author
   - ○ **A.** color
   - ○ **B.** writer
   - ○ **C.** story
   - ○ **D.** singer

4. bright student
   - ○ **A.** shiny
   - ○ **B.** tall
   - ○ **C.** smart
   - ○ **D.** silly

5. fry a hamburger
   - ○ **A.** eat
   - ○ **B.** cook
   - ○ **C.** share
   - ○ **D.** taste

6. rotating earth
   - ○ **A.** turning
   - ○ **B.** falling
   - ○ **C.** slowing
   - ○ **D.** glowing

7. challenging problem
   - ○ **A.** ugly
   - ○ **B.** hard
   - ○ **C.** easy
   - ○ **D.** new

Antonyms

Read the underlined word in each phrase. Mark the word below it that means the opposite or nearly the opposite.

Sample:

cheerful child
- ○ **A.** happy
- ○ **B.** pretty
- ○ **C.** sleepy
- ○ **D.** sad

1. calm lake
   - ○ **A.** dry
   - ○ **B.** large
   - ○ **C.** stormy
   - ○ **D.** quiet

2. chilly breeze
   - ○ **A.** warm
   - ○ **B.** strong
   - ○ **C.** slight
   - ○ **D.** icy

3. contest champion
   - ○ **A.** umpire
   - ○ **B.** loser
   - ○ **C.** player
   - ○ **D.** winner

4. enjoy the movie
   - ○ **A.** watch
   - ○ **B.** show
   - ○ **C.** like
   - ○ **D.** dislike

5. recall her name
   - ○ **A.** forget
   - ○ **B.** remember
   - ○ **C.** say
   - ○ **D.** listen

6. shrinking in size
   - ○ **A.** shopping
   - ○ **B.** teasing
   - ○ **C.** changing
   - ○ **D.** growing

7. wobbly legs
   - ○ **A.** young
   - ○ **B.** short
   - ○ **C.** sturdy
   - ○ **D.** old

Reading Skills Practice Test 12

READING COMPREHENSION

Read each story. Then fill in the circle that best completes each sentence or answers each question.

SAMPLE

> John Chapman loved apple trees. He walked hundreds of miles around the country. He always carried a bag of apple seeds with him. He gave farmers seeds to **plant**. John also planted seeds as he walked. He was called Johnny Appleseed.

I. What is the best title for this story?
- ○ **A.** "How to Plant Seeds"
- ○ **B.** "Johnny Appleseed"
- ○ **C.** "A Tall Apple Tree"
- ○ **D.** "Fruits of the World"

2. In this story, the word **plant** means
- ○ **A.** a factory.
- ○ **B.** a young tree.
- ○ **C.** to put in the ground.
- ○ **D.** fields.

A. Can you imagine wearing an outfit made of garbage? It could happen! A few companies across the country are making clothes from things people throw away. For example, one company makes sweaters from old soda bottles. First, plastic bottles are cut into small pieces. The pieces are melted. Then the melted plastic is stretched into long, thin yarn. The yarn is used to make fluffy sweaters. Many people think these new "recycled" clothes can help us cut down on trash.

I. What can be used to make sweaters?
- ○ **A.** bags
- ○ **B.** bottles
- ○ **C.** cups
- ○ **D.** shoes

2. What happens first?
- ○ **A.** Pieces are melted.
- ○ **B.** Sweaters are sold.
- ○ **C.** Bottles are cut up.
- ○ **D.** Yarn is made.

3. The author wrote this story to
- ○ **A.** sell clothes.
- ○ **B.** explain how yarn is made.
- ○ **C.** show how trash can be recycled.
- ○ **D.** tell why plastic is harmful.

B. Large parts of southern California are dry, desert areas. Very little rain falls there. Only northern California gets much rain or snow.

Most people in California live in big cities in the south. So people have found ways to move water from the north to these dry **locations**. They collect rainwater in man-made lakes called reservoirs. Then they use waterways and large pipes to move the water across long distances.

1. This story is mainly about
   - ○ **A.** water in California.
   - ○ **B.** lakes in California.
   - ○ **C.** how to build waterways.
   - ○ **D.** rainfall in the U.S.

2. In this story, the word **locations** means
   - ○ **A.** states.   ○ **C.** rivers.
   - ○ **B.** places.   ○ **D.** people.

3. You can guess that
   - ○ **A.** California is very small.
   - ○ **B.** California is large.
   - ○ **C.** California has few cities.
   - ○ **D.** it is easy to move water.

C. Long ago in Persia, a man owned 117,000 books. He took his books everywhere. But it was not easy. He had to stack them on the backs of 400 camels! The camels carried the books in alphabetical order across deserts and through small towns. When the man wanted a new book, he paid townspeople to find one for him.

1. What is the best title for this story?
   - ○ **A.** "Desert Camels"
   - ○ **B.** "The Traveling Library"
   - ○ **C.** "Persia Today"
   - ○ **D.** "How to Find Books"

2. How many books did the man in the story own?
   - ○ **A.** 400
   - ○ **B.** 100,000
   - ○ **C.** 17,000
   - ○ **D.** 117,000

D. Firefighters risk their lives to save others. When an alarm sounds, these brave workers rush to the scene of a fire. They put out the flames by shooting water from long hoses. They crawl into burning buildings to save trapped people. They even cut through roofs and walls to get at the fire.

1. You can guess from this story that
   - ○ **A.** firefighters have important jobs.
   - ○ **B.** smoking causes all fires.
   - ○ **C.** most fires happen in houses.
   - ○ **D.** water does not help to put out fires.

2. Which of these is an *opinion* about firefighters?
   - ○ **A.** They use hoses.
   - ○ **B.** They save people's lives.
   - ○ **C.** They ride on fire trucks.
   - ○ **D.** They have fun jobs.

E. Many years ago, the U.S. Navy put microphones on the ocean floor. The microphones picked up noises in the water. Scientists listened to the sounds to try to figure out what kinds of ships were in the water. But the scientists **detected** other noises too. Some of the noises were made by whales!

Whales make noises to "talk" to each other. Each kind of whale makes a different noise. Now scientists are using microphones to study whales. They are listening to the whale noises to count how many whales are in the oceans. The scientists want to find out which kinds of whales are endangered.

I. This story's main idea is that
 ○ **A.** hunters kill whales.
 ○ **B.** the Navy watches ships.
 ○ **C.** oceans have many animals.
 ○ **D.** microphones are being used to study whales.

2. In this story, the word **detected** means
 ○ **A.** saw.   ○ **C.** heard.
 ○ **B.** sent.   ○ **D.** added.

3. You can guess that
 ○ **A.** whales talk to people.
 ○ **B.** some kinds of whales are in danger.
 ○ **C.** microphones are new.
 ○ **D.** whales are afraid of ships.

F. Taking care of your teeth is important. It can help prevent tooth decay and gum disease. Good tooth care includes brushing and flossing every day, visiting your dentist, and eating healthful foods. To brush your teeth, follow these steps:
1. Get a toothbrush with soft bristles.
2. Place a small amount of toothpaste on the brush. A toothpaste with fluoride is best.
3. Place the toothbrush against your teeth at an angle.
4. To brush the front and back of your teeth, move the brush back and forth or in small circles.
5. Scrub back and forth on the part of your teeth you use to chew.
6. Brush your tongue to remove tiny **particles** of food.
7. Rinse your mouth with water or mouthwash.

I. In this story, the word **particles** means
 ○ **A.** colors.   ○ **C.** bites.
 ○ **B.** pieces.   ○ **D.** eats.

2. Before brushing, you should
 ○ **A.** rinse with mouthwash.
 ○ **B.** wash your face.
 ○ **C.** drink cold water.
 ○ **D.** get fluoride toothpaste.

3. Poor tooth care can cause
 ○ **A.** a bad diet.
 ○ **B.** soft bristles on your toothbrush.
 ○ **C.** healthy teeth.
 ○ **D.** gum disease.

4. This story would probably go on to talk about
 ○ **A.** visiting the dentist.
 ○ **B.** taking care of your ears.
 ○ **C.** cleaning your sink.
 ○ **D.** how animals chew.

Study Skills

Reading a Table of Contents

This table of contents is from a book called *Maple City*. The table tells what you will find in the book.

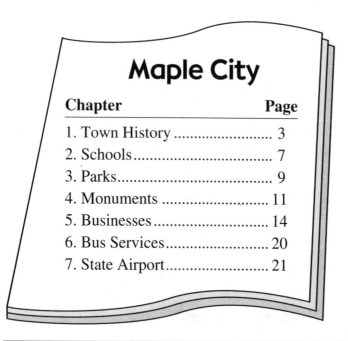

I. This book is about
○ **A.** history.   ○ **C.** Maple City.
○ **B.** parks.   ○ **D.** buses.

2. Chapter 3 starts on
○ **A.** page 7.   ○ **C.** page 11.
○ **B.** page 9.   ○ **D.** page 14.

3. How many pages are in chapter 5?
○ **A.** three   ○ **C.** five
○ **B.** four   ○ **D.** six

4. When was Maple City first built? You might find out on
○ **A.** pages 3–6.
○ **B.** pages 11–13.
○ **C.** pages 14–19.
○ **D.** page 21.

Reading a Pictograph

This pictograph shows how many dogs and cats live in Maple City.

Pets in Maple City

Street	Cats	Dogs
Oak Street	🐱 🐱	🐶
Elm Street	🐱 🐱	🐶 🐶
Walnut Street		🐶
Pine Street	🐱	🐶

Key: 🐱 = 5 Cats   🐶 = 5 Dogs

I. The number of pets on Elm Street is
○ **A.** 4.   ○ **C.** 10.
○ **B.** 5.   ○ **D.** 20.

2. The street with 15 pets is
○ **A.** Pine.   ○ **C.** Oak.
○ **B.** Walnut.   ○ **D.** Elm.

3. The street with fewer than 10 pets is
○ **A.** Pine.   ○ **C.** Oak.
○ **B.** Walnut.   ○ **D.** Elm.

4. In Maple City, there are
○ **A.** the same number of cats as dogs.
○ **B.** more cats than dogs.
○ **C.** more dogs than cats.
○ **D.** too many cats and dogs.

Reading Skills Practice Test 13

READING COMPREHENSION

Read each story. Then fill in the circle that best completes each sentence or answers each question.

Did you ever wonder why your mouth waters when you smell supper cooking or spot a fresh-baked batch of cookies? When you smell or see the food, your senses send a signal to your brain that it's time to eat. Then your brain tells your mouth to start making watery saliva. When you finally take a bite of food, this saliva will make the food **moist**. Wet food is easier to chew and swallow.

1. What is the best title for this story?
- ○ **A.** "How to Bake Cookies"
- ○ **B.** "How Your Brain Works"
- ○ **C.** "Why Your Mouth Waters"
- ○ **D.** "Tasty Treats Around the World"

2. In this story, the word **moist** means
- ○ **A.** wet.
- ○ **B.** spicy.
- ○ **C.** cold.
- ○ **D.** hot.

A. Police dogs have an important role in fighting crime. Each dog works closely with one police officer. Together, the dog and the officer go through four months of difficult training. Once the training is complete, the dog uses its super-powerful nose to help the officer track down criminals, search for stolen property, and sniff out drugs and other illegal substances. A police dog and its human partner always work as a team. In most cases, a dog even lives at home with its human partner! This helps to keep the **bond** between them strong.

1. This story is mainly about
- ○ **A.** fighting crime.
- ○ **B.** police dogs.
- ○ **C.** dogs' sense of smell.
- ○ **D.** which dogs make the best pets.

2. In this story, the word **bond** means
- ○ **A.** battle.
- ○ **B.** job.
- ○ **C.** connection.
- ○ **D.** house.

3. A police dog does *not*
- ○ **A.** track down criminals.
- ○ **B.** live at the police station.
- ○ **C.** sniff out drugs.
- ○ **D.** go through training.

4. You can guess from the story that
- ○ **A.** dogs' noses are stronger than humans'.
- ○ **B.** all police officers have police dogs.
- ○ **C.** police-dog training is easy.
- ○ **D.** police officers and their dogs get tired of one another.

B. Spring comes every year—and so do insects! Each year when the weather gets warmer, gardens, meadows, fields, and forests fill with bugs. There are at least one million different species of insects—more than any other kind of animal. Some of them are as big as the palm of your hand, while others are too small to be seen without a microscope.

Despite their differences, all insects share a few important characteristics. For example, they all have six legs and three body parts—a head, a thorax, and an abdomen. They also all have an *exoskeleton*, or skeleton on the outside of their body instead of on the inside. This exoskeleton looks like a hard shell. Its job is to protect an insect's delicate digestive system and other internal organs.

1. This story is mainly about
   - ○ **A.** using a microscope.
   - ○ **B.** characteristics of insects.
   - ○ **C.** spring weather.
   - ○ **D.** insects in fields and forests.

2. You can guess from the story that an eight-legged spider is
   - ○ **A.** a large insect.
   - ○ **B.** not an insect.
   - ○ **C.** a forest insect
   - ○ **D.** very rare.

3. An insect needs an exoskeleton because
   - ○ **A.** it has only three body parts.
   - ○ **B.** it lives in extremely hot places.
   - ○ **C.** its legs are long.
   - ○ **D.** its internal organs are delicate.

4. Which of these is an *opinion* about insects?
   - ○ **A.** They can live in fields.
   - ○ **B.** They come in many sizes.
   - ○ **C.** They are very creepy.
   - ○ **D.** They have six legs.

C. A family vacation is a lot of fun, but getting to your vacation spot can be boring! There's nothing like sitting in a car for hours at a time to make a person grouchy and groggy. The next time your family takes a long road trip, try playing one of these traditional travel games. Families have been enjoying them for decades!

- **License Plate Game:** To play this game, give each player a pencil and pad of paper. Then try to spot license plates from different states. Whoever finds the most states wins.
- **Beep:** Pick a certain **model** of car (for example, pickup trucks or station wagons) at the start of your trip. Each time you spot that type of car, say "beep" and the color of the vehicle you saw. The first person to say "beep" gets one point. The first person to get 10 points wins the game.

1. What is the best title for this story?
   - ○ **A.** "License Plates"
   - ○ **B.** "Fun Travel Games"
   - ○ **C.** "Long Road Trips"
   - ○ **D.** "How to Win at "Beep"

2. In this story the word **model** means
   - ○ **A.** beauty.
   - ○ **B.** size.
   - ○ **C.** type.
   - ○ **D.** truck.

3. To play the license-plate game, what should you do first?
   - ○ **A.** Pick a type of car.
   - ○ **B.** Get one point.
   - ○ **C.** Look for plates from different states.
   - ○ **D.** Give out pencils and paper.

4. A person wins at "Beep" when he or she
   - ○ **A.** gets 1 point.
   - ○ **B.** gets 10 points.
   - ○ **C.** gets more states than everyone else.
   - ○ **D.** gets all 50 states.

D. Monday

I overslept and missed my bus.
I didn't have time to eat.
I wore plaid pants with polka dots
And my sneakers on the wrong feet.

I **trudged** to school in the rain
And got there just in time
To hear the teacher announce a test
On math chapters one through nine.

When teacher asked if we had questions,
I raised my hand and said,
"I'm not quite ready for today.
May I please go back to bed?"

By Karen Kellaher

1. Another good title for this poem might be
   ○ **A.** "Math Test."
   ○ **B.** "My Bad Day."
   ○ **C.** "I Missed the Train."
   ○ **D.** "Saturday Morning."

2. In this poem, the word **trudged** means
   ○ **A.** few.   ○ **C.** dressed.
   ○ **B.** overslept.   ○ **D.** walked.

3. The poet probably created this rhyme to
   ○ **A.** entertain children.
   ○ **B.** make teachers angry.
   ○ **C.** complain about weekends.
   ○ **D.** celebrate a holiday.

4. You can guess that the child in the poem
   ○ **A.** is not hungry for breakfast.
   ○ **B.** needs to buy new sneakers.
   ○ **C.** didn't study for the math test.
   ○ **D.** looks good in plaid.

E.

Today, many doctors are women, but that was not always the case. Until the middle of the 19th century, only men were permitted to become doctors. A determined woman named Elizabeth Blackwell thought that was unfair— and changed the course of history.

Elizabeth Blackwell was born in England in 1821. She moved to the United States with her family when she was a teenager. When she was 23 years old, Blackwell decided to become a doctor. The smart young woman applied to many medical schools, but was told "no" again and again. Finally, three years later, a small school in New York accepted Blackwell. Professors at the school never believed she would show up for classes. But Blackwell showed up and studied hard. She graduated at the head of her class.

Once she had her medical degree, Blackwell cared for many patients. She even opened a special hospital for women and children. Years later, she moved back to England and helped women there break into the medical field.

1. What did Blackwell do last?
   ○ **A.** She opened a hospital.
   ○ **B.** She applied to medical school.
   ○ **C.** She moved to England.
   ○ **D.** She moved to the U.S.

2. This story would probably go on to talk about
   ○ **A.** Elizabeth Blackwell's family.
   ○ **B.** how things have changed for female doctors.
   ○ **C.** how to get into medical school.
   ○ **D.** why Blackwell decided to become a doctor.

3. Which of these is a *fact* about Blackwell?
   ○ **A.** She was an amazing woman.
   ○ **B.** She was a doctor.
   ○ **C.** She was smarter than most male doctors.
   ○ **D.** She was probably not very bright.

4. You might find this story in
   ○ **A.** an atlas.
   ○ **B.** a nature encyclopedia.
   ○ **C.** a book of biographies.
   ○ **D.** a book of poems.

VOCABULARY
Which Word Is Missing?

In each of the following paragraphs, a word is missing. First, read the paragraph. Then find the missing word in the list of words beneath the paragraph. Fill in the circle next to the word that is missing.

Sample:

When I awoke Saturday morning, I had hoped to spend the day in the park. Then I glanced out the window and saw the day was rainy and _____ . So much for my big plans!

- ○ **A.** sunny
- ○ **B.** long
- ○ **C.** foggy
- ○ **D.** bright

Instead, I decided to stay inside. I put some water in the _____ to make a cup of tea and settled down with a good book.

- ○ **A.** window
- ○ **B.** kettle
- ○ **C.** sink
- ○ **D.** tub

I. Everyone knows that manners are important, but sometimes we all need a reminder. Here are some simple things you can do to be _____ .

- ○ **A.** polite
- ○ **B.** first
- ○ **C.** rude
- ○ **D.** sweet

2. At the dinner table, you should always use a fork, spoon, and knife to eat your food. And keep in mind that chewing with your mouth open is _____ !

- ○ **A.** difficult
- ○ **B.** lovely
- ○ **C.** tasty
- ○ **D.** impolite

3. If you would like a dish that is at the other end of the table, it is better not to reach for it yourself. Kindly ask someone else to pass the item to you. And don't forget to say "thank you" _____ .

- ○ **A.** loudly
- ○ **B.** afterward
- ○ **C.** first
- ○ **D.** slowly

4. When answering the telephone at home, don't just pick up the line and mutter, "yo." Instead, _____ the person in a cheerful voice and ask who is calling.

- ○ **A.** request
- ○ **B.** mind
- ○ **C.** greet
- ○ **D.** dismiss

5. Good manners are important at school, too. When the teacher or another student is speaking, let him or her finish before you respond. No one likes to be _____ .

- ○ **A.** boring
- ○ **B.** answered
- ○ **C.** sad
- ○ **D.** interrupted

6. If you accidentally bump into someone in line in the cafeteria, make sure the person is not hurt. Also, remember to say, "_____ me." This will show that you did not mean to be rude.

- ○ **A.** watch
- ○ **B.** embarrass
- ○ **C.** excuse
- ○ **D.** dear

7. These pointers tell you what to do in a variety of situations. But above all, keep in mind that having good manners means being considerate of others around you. If you remember that, you'll find that others will truly enjoy your _____ .

- ○ **A.** jokes
- ○ **B.** company
- ○ **C.** stories
- ○ **D.** smile

Reading Skills Practice Test 14

READING COMPREHENSION

Read each story. Then fill in the circle that best completes each sentence or answers each question.

SAMPLE

Thanksgiving has been around for over 350 years. That's when Pilgrims and Native Americans **dined** together. But this holiday has changed a lot! For example, potatoes are a hit today. But the Pilgrims had never even heard of potatoes! And apples were not yet grown in America, so there was no apple pie.

I. What is the best title for this story?
○ **A.** "Thanksgiving Then and Now"
○ **B.** "Favorite Foods of the Pilgrims"
○ **C.** "Why Thanksgiving Has Always Been the Same"
○ **D.** "Home for the Holidays"

2. In this story, the word **dined** means
○ **A.** worked.
○ **B.** planted.
○ **C.** ate.
○ **D.** sang.

A. Students at Table Mound Elementary in Iowa knew all about recycling and other ways to help the Earth. So, they decided to teach the rest of their community about Earth Day. First, they borrowed 500 big brown paper bags from a local food store. Then, they decorated the bags with Earth Day messages and pictures. Later, the kids **returned** the bags to the store. Shoppers used the bags to take home their groceries.

I. This story is mainly about
○ **A.** ways to save money on groceries.
○ **B.** Earth Day celebrations around the country.
○ **C.** one school's Earth Day project.
○ **D.** art projects using brown bags.

2. In this story, the word **returned** means
○ **A.** took back.
○ **B.** sold.
○ **C.** took away.
○ **D.** shopped.

3. What happened first?
○ **A.** Students decorated brown bags.
○ **B.** Students borrowed bags from a store.
○ **C.** Shoppers used the decorated bags.
○ **D.** Students returned bags to the store.

4. You can guess from the story that
○ **A.** People in Iowa buy lots of groceries.
○ **B.** Students at Table Mound Elementary are good artists.
○ **C.** The bags taught shoppers about Earth Day.
○ **D.** Shoppers in Iowa love the Earth.

B.   An area called Patagonia, in Argentina, was home to some of the largest dinosaurs that ever lived. Fernando Novas is a scientist who studies dinosaur bones. He says, "The giants of all giants lived here." One of them, the Giganotosaurus, was a meat-eating monster. It was about 45 feet long and weighed 8 to 10 tons. Another huge dinosaur was called the Argentinosaurus. It was about 100 feet long and weighed 100 tons. It was no meat-eating monster, though. The Argentinosaurus was an **herbivore**. In other words, it ate only plants.

I.   Which is the name of a giant dinosaur?
○ **A.** Patagonia   ○ **C.** Argentina
○ **B.** Argentinosaurus   ○ **D.** Novas

2.   What is the main idea of this story?
○ **A.** Some of the largest dinosaurs ever lived in Patagonia.
○ **B.** Fernando Novas is a scientist who studied dinosaur bones.
○ **C.** The Giganotosaurus ate huge amounts of meat.
○ **D.** Some dinosaurs were quite small.

3.   In this story, the word **herbivore** means
○ **A.** meat eater.   ○ **C.** scientist.
○ **B.** giant dinosaur.   ○ **D.** plant eater.

4.   How large was the Giganotosaurus?
○ **A.** about 100 feet long
○ **B.** over 500 feet long
○ **C.** about 45 feet long
○ **D.** less than 30 feet long

C.   It's amazing what you can create from a field of maize, or corn. One summer, a farmer in Walden, New York, turned his cornfield into a giant maze! To make the maze, farmer Richard Hodgson planted rows and rows of corn. Then, when the corn was about 10 inches high, farm workers carefully pulled out some of the corn plants. That made a maze pattern in the fields. By late summer, the corn maze was 8 feet high and ready for visitors.

Hundreds of people explored Hodgson's maze. Most people took a whole hour to find their way out. Each group of explorers was given a tall flag. If they got lost, they waved the flag and someone went to help. The maze shut down at the end of the summer. The corn was used to feed farm animals.

I.   What is the best title for this story?
○ **A.** "How to Grow Tall Corn"
○ **B.** "A Farm in New York"
○ **C.** "What to Feed Farm Animals"
○ **D.** "An Amazing Maze of Maize"

2.   The maze was ready for visitors when the corn was
○ **A.** about 10 inches high.
○ **B.** about 8 feet high.
○ **C.** waving tall flags.
○ **D.** planted in rows.

3.   Which happened last?
○ **A.** Hodgson pulled out some corn plants.
○ **B.** Hodgson planted rows of corn.
○ **C.** The corn was fed to farm animals.
○ **D.** The corn plants grew 10 inches high.

4.   You can guess from the story that
○ **A.** few visitors came to the maze.
○ **B.** the maze was pretty hard to go through.
○ **C.** the maze was really simple.
○ **D.** everyone who entered the maze got lost.

D. The next time you munch on a peanut-butter sandwich, say thanks to George Washington Carver. This African-American scientist invented hundreds of products, including everyone's favorite sandwich spread.

Carver was born around 1860. He became an expert in science and farming. In 1897, he learned that farmers in the Southern U.S. were having a problem. These farmers grew a lot of cotton, and the cotton plants were ruining their **soil.**

Carver offered to help. He discovered that planting peanuts every other year would make the soil rich again. Southern farmers began planting peanuts, and the problem was solved.

But soon, there was a new problem. The farmers fed the peanuts to their cows, but there were still many peanuts left over. Carver got to work. He invented 325 different ways to use peanuts. Soon, people were using peanuts to make everything from cooking oil to ink—and, of course, peanut butter!

I. In the story, the word **soil** means
 ○ **A.** peanut.   ○ **C.** cotton.
 ○ **B.** dirt.   ○ **D.** plant.

2. Farmers started growing many peanuts because peanut plants
 ○ **A.** grew very quickly.
 ○ **B.** were easy to find.
 ○ **C.** were good for the soil.
 ○ **D.** were cheaper than cotton.

3. Which of these is an *opinion*?
 ○ **A.** Peanut butter is delicious.
 ○ **B.** Carver was born around 1860.
 ○ **C.** Farmers fed peanuts to their cows.
 ○ **D.** Peanuts grow on plants.

E. Way back when, the Sun and the Moon were very good friends with the Sea. Every day, Sun and Moon visited Sea. They talked and laughed and had a good time. But Sea never visited Sun and Moon, and that hurt their feelings.

Finally, Sun and Moon asked Sea why he never visited. "Your house is not big enough," said Sea. "You would need to build a very, very, big house for me to visit."

So Sun and Moon built a huge house. It was so big that it took a whole day to walk from one end to the other. Sun and Moon felt **confident** that Sea would fit.

The next day, Sea visited. He flowed into the house until the water was waist high. "Should I stop?" he asked.

"No, no," said Sun and Moon. "Come on in." So Sea kept flowing. Soon, he reached the ceiling. Sun and Moon had to sit on the roof. Finally, the whole house was underwater, including the roof. Sun and Moon had to leap onto a cloud floating by. And that's how Sun and Moon came to live in the sky.

I. In this story, the word **confident** means
 ○ **A.** scared.   ○ **C.** huge.
 ○ **B.** sure.   ○ **D.** ocean.

2. Sun and Moon leaped onto a cloud
 ○ **A.** because they were angry at Sea.
 ○ **B.** because their new house was too big.
 ○ **C.** to stay above water.
 ○ **D.** to visit friends in the sky.

3. This story might go on to tell about
 ○ **A.** the biggest house in the world.
 ○ **B.** tips for water safety.
 ○ **C.** more adventures of Sun and Moon.
 ○ **D.** eclipses.

VOCABULARY
Which Word Is Missing?

In each of the following paragraphs, a word is missing. First, read the paragraph. Then find the missing word in the list of words beneath the paragraph. Fill in the circle next to the word that is missing.

Sample:

I'm going to take a walk in the rain. But first, I'll grab my _____. I don't want to get wet.

- ○ **A.** book
- ○ **B.** sweater
- ○ **C.** umbrella
- ○ **D.** socks

I had a really large lunch today. I ate two sandwiches, an apple, and a ____ slice of cake. I felt very full by the time I finished all that cake.

- ○ **A.** tiny
- ○ **B.** thick
- ○ **C.** fruit
- ○ **D.** piece

I. Some tigers live in zoos around the world. But tigers in the wild are found only in Asia. In the wild, tigers live in grassy, wooded areas. At one time, about 100,000 tigers roamed the _____ of Asia.

- ○ **A.** cities
- ○ **B.** China
- ○ **C.** forests
- ○ **D.** deserts

2. The Siberian tiger is the world's _____ tiger. It weighs about 500 pounds and is over eight and a half feet tall. The smallest tiger is the Sumatran tiger. It weighs about 250 pounds and is eight feet long.

- ○ **A.** largest
- ○ **B.** pounds
- ○ **C.** fastest
- ○ **D.** heavy

3. Today, tigers are _____ in number. There are only 7,500 tigers left in the wild. In fact, tigers are in danger of dying out.

- ○ **A.** size
- ○ **B.** growing
- ○ **C.** dead
- ○ **D.** shrinking

4. What's happening to the mighty tiger? One problem is that tigers are losing their _____. People have built villages and farms on the land where tigers lived. They have destroyed tiger habitats.

- ○ **A.** homes
- ○ **B.** speed
- ○ **C.** stripes
- ○ **D.** cubs

5. Another problem is hunters. They kill the tigers to make medicine from their bones and to sell the beautiful tiger skins. It is _____ to hunt tigers. But many people break the law.

- ○ **A.** exciting
- ○ **B.** illegal
- ○ **C.** scary
- ○ **D.** boring

6. Who caused the tiger problem? People caused it. Now, it is up to people to ____ the problem. If we don't do something to help tigers they will surely become extinct.

- ○ **A.** cause
- ○ **B.** hide
- ○ **C.** fix
- ○ **D.** write

7. Tiger experts around the world want to help tigers. They had a big meeting in Texas to talk about ways to stop tigers from dying out. School children are also working to keep tigers safe. Schools in the U.S. have raised thousands of dollars to _____ tigers.

- ○ **A.** hunt
- ○ **B.** pet
- ○ **C.** spend
- ○ **D.** save

Reading Skills Practice Test 15

READING COMPREHENSION

Read each story. Then fill in the circle that best completes each sentence or answers each question.

SAMPLE

Some vegetables, such as broccoli, contain nutrients that may help to **prevent** diseases. But many kids don't like to eat these vegetables. Now researchers are looking for ways to make veggies fun. They are trying to create doughnuts and other snacks that contain vegetables.

1. What is the best title for this story?
○ **A.** "My Favorite Vegetables"
○ **B.** "Making Veggies Fun"
○ **C.** "Doughnuts Are Delicious"
○ **D.** "Why Broccoli Tastes Bad"

2. In this story, the word **prevent** means
○ **A.** eat.
○ **B.** fry.
○ **C.** keep away.
○ **D.** melt.

A. Are you scared of heights? Fifteen-year-old Merrick Johnston is not. In 1995, she climbed Mount McKinley—a 20,320-foot mountain in Alaska. She became the youngest person ever to reach the mountain's **peak**! Merrick climbed with her mom and a guide. They each carried a backpack full of supplies. The team faced icy slopes and rough weather. It took 26 days to reach the top.

1. What is the main idea of this story?
○ **A.** Merrick reached a tough goal at a young age.
○ **B.** Fear of heights is a serious problem.
○ **C.** Merrick carried a backpack.
○ **D.** Weather can be a problem for mountain climbers.

2. In this story, the word **peak** means
○ **A.** bottom.
○ **B.** rocky.
○ **C.** top.
○ **D.** snow.

3. Mount McKinley is
○ **A.** less than 20,000 feet tall.
○ **B.** 26 days old.
○ **C.** a mountain in Alabama.
○ **D.** more than 20,000 feet tall.

4. You can guess from the story that
○ **A.** Mount McKinley is the world's tallest mountain.
○ **B.** the weather is usually mild on Mount McKinley.
○ **C.** Merrick's guide was older than she was.
○ **D.** Merrick's guide was 13 years old.

B.   People have been flying kites for 3,000 years. During that time, kites have served many purposes. The Chinese were the first kite makers. One story says that Chinese soldiers attached bamboo pipes to their kites. As wind passed through the pipes, it made a whistling sound that scared away enemies! In 1752, Ben Franklin used a kite to study lightning. And in the early 1900s, the Wright brothers used kites to help design the first airplane.

I.   What did Chinese soldiers attach to their kites?
○ **A.** lightning rods
○ **B.** bamboo pipes
○ **C.** silver flutes
○ **D.** box kites

2.   This story is mostly about
○ **A.** kites as weapons of war.
○ **B.** the history of bamboo.
○ **C.** the many ways kites have been used.
○ **D.** Ben Franklin.

3.   Which happened last?
○ **A.** The Wright brothers used kites.
○ **B.** The Chinese began making kites.
○ **C.** Ben Franklin studied lightning.
○ **D.** Chinese soldiers used kites in battle.

4.   You can guess from this story that
○ **A.** Chinese soldiers won many battles.
○ **B.** kites have always been just for kids.
○ **C.** kites have had many uses.
○ **D.** Ben Franklin owned many kites.

C.   Long ago, an Ojibway Indian named Wenibojo went on a long trip to the forest. When he got hungry, he dug up the roots of a bush and ate them. The roots tasted good, but they made him sick.

Wenibojo looked for something better to eat. Suddenly he heard the sound of ducks nearby. He followed the sounds to a beautiful lake, where the ducks were eating plants. Wenibojo tasted one. It was wild rice! He returned to his village to tell the people there about the special food.

The Ojibway still harvest rice today, but only as much as they need. They always leave some so that the ducks can eat.

I.   Wenibojo was led to the lake by the
○ **A.** sound of ducks nearby.
◐ **B.** smell of wild rice cooking.
○ **C.** sight of ducks eating plants.
○ **D.** sound of waves crashing.

2.   What is the best title for this story?
○ **A.** "Wenibojo's Adventures in the Forest"
○ **B.** "Why Ducks Like Wild Rice"
○ **C.** "How the Ojibway Discovered Wild Rice"
◉ **D.** "The Eating Habits of the Ojibway"

3.   The author probably told this story
○ **A.** to warn people about eating roots.
○ **B.** to tell about a part of the Ojibway heritage.
○ **C.** to tell people to eat more wild rice.
○ **D.** to tell people to be nice to ducks.

4.   You can guess from this story that
○ **A.** wild rice grows on plants.
◐ **B.** wild rice is harvested from the roots of a bush.
○ **C.** ducks are smarter than people.
◐ **D.** the Ojibway people eat wild rice only on special occasions.

D.   Frogs have lived on this planet for millions of years. But recently, scientists have noticed that certain types of frogs are disappearing. Some species have even become extinct. What's the problem? Experts have two **theories**:

- Ruined homes: Many frogs live in ponds or other wet areas. People have dried up these areas in order to build roads or buildings. Some other frogs live in forests. Many forests have been destroyed so that people can use the land. That leaves fewer places for frogs to live.
- Pollution: Chemicals get into the ponds and lands where many frogs live. Some scientists say the chemicals make frogs sick.

I.   In this story, the word **theories** means
- ○ **A.** scientists.
- ○ **B.** lily pads.
- ○ **C.** habitats.
- ○ **D.** ideas.

2.   This story is mostly about
- ○ **A.** why frogs are disappearing.
- ○ **B.** where frogs live.
- ○ **C.** scientists who study frogs.
- ○ **D.** pollution.

3.   Frogs have fewer places to live because
- ○ **A.** scientists have chased them away.
- ○ **B.** oceans have dried up.
- ○ **C.** people have destroyed their homes.
- ○ **D.** too many baby frogs have been born.

4.   Which of these is an *opinion*?
- ○ **A.** Some frogs lose their homes when ponds are dried up.
- ○ **B.** People should never destroy frogs' homes.
- ○ **C.** Some types of frogs have become extinct.
- ○ **D.** Some frogs live in forests.

E. The Old Lady Who Swallowed a Fly

I know an old lady who swallowed a fly.
I don't know why she swallowed a fly.
Perhaps she'll die.

I know on old lady who swallowed a spider.
It wiggled, and jiggled, and tickled inside her.
She swallowed the spider to catch the fly.
I don't know why she swallowed the fly.
Maybe she'll die.

I know an old lady who swallowed a bird.
How absurd to swallow a bird!
She swallowed the bird to catch the spider
That wiggled, and jiggled, and tickled
      inside her.
She swallowed the spider to catch the fly.
I don't know why she swallowed the fly.
I guess she'll die.

I.   In this song, the word **perhaps** means
- ○ **A.** definitely.
- ○ **C.** unlikely.
- ○ **B.** maybe.
- ○ **D.** always.

2.   The second item the old lady swallowed was
- ○ **A.** a bird.
- ○ **C.** a spider.
- ○ **B.** a fly.
- ○ **D.** a rat.

3.   The next verse will probably tell
- ○ **A.** why the old lady swallowed the fly.
- ○ **B.** where the old lady lived.
- ○ **C.** what the lady ate to catch the bird.
- ○ **D.** what flies and spiders eat.

4.   You would probably find this song in
- ○ **A.** a book of rock songs.
- ○ **B.** a book about insects.
- ○ **C.** a children's songbook.
- ○ **D.** a cookbook.

VOCABULARY
Which Word Is Missing?

In each of the following paragraphs, a word is missing. First, read the paragraph. Then find the missing word in the list of words beneath the paragraph. Fill in the circle next to the word that is missing.

Sample:

I want to go for a bike ride. But first, I'll put on my _____ . It is not safe to ride without one.

- ○ **A.** book
- ○ **B.** raincoat
- ○ **C.** shoes
- ○ **D.** helmet

It can be hard work to ride a bicycle uphill. Yesterday, I rode up a very _____ hill. I was really tired when I finally got to the top.

- ○ **A.** short
- ○ **B.** steep
- ○ **C.** heavy
- ○ **D.** fast

I. Cheetahs live on the plains of Africa. Like the lion and the _____ , the cheetah is a cat. But don't be fooled: Cheetahs are a lot bigger and faster than your pet kitten at home!

- ○ **A.** dog
- ○ **B.** leopard
- ○ **C.** house
- ○ **D.** zebra

2. Cheetahs are meat eaters. That means they have to _____ and kill smaller animals to survive. Cheetahs often hunt gazelles.

- ○ **A.** wash
- ○ **B.** ride
- ○ **C.** stalk
- ○ **D.** defend

3. The gazelle is an animal that looks a little like a deer. Gazelles are very fast runners. Luckily for the cheetah, it is even more _____ than a gazelle. Once a cheetah gets close to a gazelle, it can easily catch the creature and eat it.

- ○ **A.** hungry
- ○ **B.** pretty
- ○ **C.** swift
- ○ **D.** spotted

4. In fact, the cheetah is the fastest land animal in the world—faster than a grizzly bear or an Olympic athlete. At top speed, a cheetah runs even faster than some people drive their cars. Luckily, drivers don't have to deal with cheetahs racing down the _____ .

- ○ **A.** cabin
- ○ **B.** highway
- ○ **C.** lawn
- ○ **D.** river

5. Another big cat—the lion—is sometimes called the King of Beasts. It lives in Africa, too. Although cheetahs are faster than lions, lions are much bigger and more powerful. What they lack in speed, they make up for in _____ . The lion really uses its muscles.

- ○ **A.** strength
- ○ **B.** smell
- ○ **C.** humor
- ○ **D.** brains

6. A lion's big _____ might mean that it's showing you its teeth. Or, it might be just tired. To stay as strong as they are, lions need a lot of rest. Sometimes, they sleep 21 hours a day!

- ○ **A.** mane
- ○ **B.** yawn
- ○ **C.** muscle
- ○ **D.** cage

7. Leopards are not as strong as lions, or as fast as cheetahs. But they have their own secret weapon. The leopard's spots help it to hunt! The spots help to hide the leopard from other animals. That way, the _____ beast can easily sneak up on its unsuspecting prey.

- ○ **A.** funny
- ○ **B.** sly
- ○ **C.** huge
- ○ **D.** wet

Answer Key

TEST 1
Sample: 1.C   2.B

Passage A
1.D   2.A   3.C   4.A

Passage B
1.B   2.D   3.B   4.A

Passage C
1.C   2.D   3.C

Passage D
1.C   2.C

Passage E
1.A   2.C   3.B   4.D

Vocabulary
Synonyms
Sample: B
1.C   2.B   3.B   4.A
5.D   6.B   7.C
Antonyms
Sample: D
1.A   2.C   3.B   4.C
5.A   6.D   7.A

TEST 2
Sample: 1.B   2.C

Passage A
1.B   2.D   3.A   4.D

Passage B
1.A   2.B   3.D   4.A

Passage C
1.C   2.A   3.C   4.A

Passage D
1.B   2.A   3.B

Passage E
1.D   2.A   3.B   4.C

Vocabulary:
Synonyms
Sample: B
1.D   2.C   3.D   4.C
5.A   6.B   7.C
Antonyms
Sample: C
1.B   2.A   3.C   4.C
5.A   6.D   7.B

TEST 3
Sample:1.C   2.A

Passage A
1.B   2.D   3.C   4.B

Passage B
1.C   2.A   3.A   4.C

Passage C
1.B   2.A   3.D   4.C

Passage D
1.B   2.C   3.A   4.D

Passage E
1.A   2.C   3.B   4.B

Vocabulary
Synonyms
Sample: A
1.C   2.A   3.D   4.B
5.D   6.B   7.D   8.C
Antonyms
Sample: A
1.C   2.D   3.A   4.D
5.B   6.B   7.C   8.A

TEST 4
Sample: 1.C   2.B

Passage A
1.A   2.D   3.B

Passage B
1.A   2.B   3.B   4.B

Passage C
1.D   2.B   3.D   4.C

Passage D
1.C   2.B   3.A   4.B

Passage E
1.D   2.B   3.C

Vocabulary
Synonyms
Sample: B
1.A   2.C   3.C   4.D
5.C   6.A   7.C
Antonyms
Sample: D
1.A   2.D   3.C   4.B
5.C   6.B   7.D

TEST 5
Sample: 1.B   2.C

Passage A
1.D   2.C   3.A   4.B

Passage B
1.B   2.D   3.A   4.B

Passage C
1.C   2.C   3.B

Passage D
1.A   2.B   3.C   4.D

Passage E
1.C   2.A   3.A   4.B

Vocabulary
Synonyms
Sample: C
1.D   2.C   3.C   4.A
5.B   6.B   7.C   8.A
Antonyms
Sample: D
1.B   2.C   3.B   4.A
5.C   6.A   7.B   8.A

TEST 6
Sample: 1.C   2.A

Passage A
1.B   2.D   3.A   4.C

Passage B
1.C   2.A   3.B

Passage C
1.C   2.C   3.A

Passage D
1.D   2.A   3.B

Passage E
1.A   2.B   3.D

Vocabulary
Sample: C; A
1.A   2.D   3.C   4.B
5.C   6.B   7.A

TEST 7
Sample: 1.C   2.A

Passage A
1.D   2.B   3.C

Passage B
1.C   2.B

Passage C
1.D   2.C   3.B

Passage D
1.C   2.B

Passage E
1.B   2.A   3.B

Passage F
1.C   2.A   3.C   4.D

Vocabulary
Synonyms
Sample: D
1.B   2.C   3.A   4.D
5.A   6.A   7.D
Multiple Meanings
Sample: A
1.C   2.D   3.A   4.B

TEST 8
Sample: 1.B   2.C

Passage A
1.C 2.B 3.D 4.A 5.B

Passage B
1.B 2.C 3.A 4.C

Passage C
1.D 2.B 3.A

Passage D
1.A 2.D 3.B 4.D

Passage E
1.B 2.D 3.C

Vocabulary
Synonyms
Sample: D
1.B 2.C 3.D 4.B
5.A 6.A 7.D 8.C
Multiple Meanings
Sample: C
1.B 2.D 3.B 4.D 5.C

TEST 9
Sample: 1.B 2.C

Passage A
1.D 2.A 3.B 4.B

Passage B
1.D 2.C 3.A 4.B

Passage C
1.B 2.A 3.D 4.C

Passage D
1.B 2.C 3.A 4.C

Passage E
1.D 2.B 3.C

Vocabulary
Synonyms
Sample: A
1.D 2.B 3.A 4.C
5.B 6.B 7.B
Multiple Meanings
Sample: B
1.D 2.C 3.A 4.B 5.A

TEST 10
Sample: 1.A 2.C

Passage A
1.B 2.C 3.B 4.D 5.A

Passage B
1.D 2.D 3.A 4.B

Passage C
1.A 2.B 3.A 4.A

Passage D
1.A 2.A 3.C 4.B

Passage E
1.A 2.C 3.A 4.C

Vocabulary
Synonyms
Sample: B
1.A 2.D 3.B 4.A
5.B 6.D 7.A 8.C
Multiple Meanings
Sample: B
1.D 2.C 3.B 4.A 5.C

TEST 11
Sample: 1.C 2.A

Passage A
1.C 2.B 3.A 4.C

Passage B
1.A 2.C 3.B 4.B

Passage C
1.C 2.B 3.A 4.C 5.D

Passage D
1.B 2.A 3.C

Passage E
1.A 2.B 3.C 4.B

Vocabulary
Synonyms
Sample: B
1.D 2.D 3.B 4.C
5.B 6.A 7.B
Antonyms
Sample: D
1.C 2.A 3.B 4.D
5.A 6.D 7.C

TEST 12
Sample: 1.B 2.C

Passage A
1.B 2.C 3.C

Passage B
1.A 2.B 3.B

Passage C
1.B 2.D

Passage D
1.A 2.D

Passage E
1.D 2.C 3.B

Passage F
1.B 2.D 3.D 4.A

Study Skills
Reading a Table of Contents
1.C 2.B 3.D 4.A
Reading a Pictograph
1.D 2.C 3.B 4.A

TEST 13
Sample: 1.C 2.A

Passage A
1.B 2.C 3.B 4.A

Passage B
1.B 2.B 3.D 4.C

Passage C
1.B 2.C 3.D 4.B

Passage D
1.B 2.D 3.A 4.C

Passage E
1.C 2.B 3.B 4.C

Vocabulary:
Which Word Is Missing?
Sample: C; B
1.A 2.D 3.B 4.C
5.D 6.C 7.B

TEST 14
Sample: 1.A 2.C

Passage A
1.C 2.A 3.B 4.C

Passage B
1.B 2.A 3.D 4.C

Passage C
1.D 2.B 3.C 4.B

Passage D
1.B 2.C 3.A

Passage E
1.B 2.C 3.C

Vocabulary:
Which Word Is Missing?
Sample: C; B
1.C 2.A 3.D 4.A
5.B 6.C 7.D

TEST 15
Sample: 1.B 2.C

Passage A
1.A 2.C 3.D 4.C

Passage B
1.B 2.C 3.A 4.C

Passage C
1.A 2.C 3.B 4.A

Passage D
1.D 2.A 3.C 4.B

Passage E
1.B 2.C 3.C 4.C

Vocabulary:
Which Word Is Missing?
Sample: D; B
1.B 2.C 3.C 4.B
5.A 6.B 7.B